SOUPS, CHOWDERS, AND STEWS

The Flavor of New England

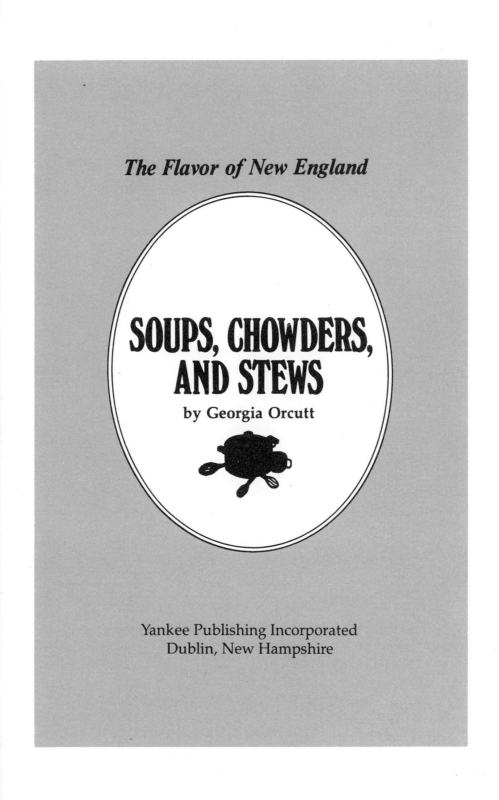

SOUPS, CHOWDERS, AND STEWS

by Georgia Orcutt

Yankee Publishing Incorporated
Dublin, New Hampshire

Designed by Carl Kirkpatrick
Illustrated by Pamela Carroll

Yankee Publishing Incorporated
Dublin, New Hampshire 03444

First edition, 1981

Seventh Printing, 1988

Copyright 1981, by Yankee Publishing Incorporated

Printed in the United States of America

Library of Congress Catalog Card No. 80-53728
ISBN 0-911658-17-3

Contents

Introduction

Soups, chowders, and stews have long played an important role in New England cookery. Bowls of steaming broth and hot chowders fortified statesman and farmer alike prior to the Revolution, and became so integral a part of the region's diet that they are still with us today.

Indeed, some recipes have become dear to the hearts of New Englanders and only a fool would suggest a change in the way they are made; a simple innovation like adding tomatoes to chowder can furrow many a Yankee's brow.

On blustery winter days, from Maine to Rhode Island, New England cooks still turn to full-bodied beef stews, rich, chunky chowders, and thick bean soups to nourish their families and friends. Come summer, influences from around the world tempt even diehard conservatives to loosen their hold on tradition and experiment with a wide range of cold soups, using fruits, spices, and cream, or yogurt, garlic, and fresh vegetables.

This book offers you a blend of tradition and innovation. There are recipes to satisfy any need — appetizer, entrée, or dessert — and to fit any season. You will find a section on preparing stock — an important beginning to homemade soup cookery — and a chapter on making croutons, noodles, dumplings, and assorted baked goods to serve with your soups, chowders, and stews. In addition, there are instructions on garnishing, cooking with herbs, and assembling useful cooking equipment.

Soups, chowders, and stews are easy to make, whether your approach to a recipe is one of strict conformity or creative abandon. And as you try these recipes or create your own versions of them, you are sure to discover that a perfectly seasoned, delicate blend of ingredients, garnished with style and served with a fresh salad and warm bread is a meal fit for a king.

Georgia Orcutt

I.
A Note on Ingredients and Cooking Equipment

Most recipes in this book call for fresh ingredients. If these are unavailable, use canned or frozen items. Frozen vegetables taste and look better than those that have been canned. Canned shrimp, clams, and packaged oysters can be disguised by a rich stock, and frozen fish or dry herbs will work when fresh are not available.

Vegetable amounts are generally given in terms of number of vegetables rather than cups. This has been done to avoid leftover raw vegetables, and the waste that often results from precise measurements of imprecise objects. Unless otherwise noted, vegetables should be of "average" size. Compensate for those that are smaller or larger than the norm.

When a recipe calls for cream, usually all-purpose whipping cream is meant. However, both light and heavy creams will work just as well. Substitute according to your personal preference or depending on how or with what the dish will be served.

GARNISHES

Garnishes add a final, gracious touch to a meal, making it all the more special. A garnish will dress up a dish that might be drab in appearance, or add an interesting contrast to an already colorful food.

Arrange packaged fish crackers into a small school atop a soup to interest children in a new recipe. Sprinkle vegetable soups with grated Parmesan, Romano, or cheddar cheese. Top individual soup servings with shredded Swiss, Gruyère, or mozzarella cheese, then place under the broiler to melt and form a chewy topping; this also adds substance to a light-bodied broth.

Chopped parsley or chives will enhance almost any soup, chowder, or stew. Or take one of the main ingredients and chop or sliver, and present on top. Toasted almonds, grated walnuts, chopped peanuts, slices of hard-boiled egg, sliced lemon, grated carrot, herb leaves, caraway seed — all of these make good garnishes.

Some of the recipes in the chapters that follow suggest a specific garnish, but these are merely ideas. Experiment with others and come up with your own favorites.

FISH

Fish are plentiful in New England, and a natural ingredient for soups, chowders, and stews. Fish stock, the basis for any good fish soup, is easily made from fish frames — skeletons and heads. Inquire at your local fish market to see when these are available. (In many communities you must get up with the birds to reach the market before its refuse is sent away.)

Combine fish stock with fresh fish when making soup, chowder, or stew. Skin the fish before cooking. Remember that fish poaches quickly in simmering liquid, and many fish can be cooked through in as little time as ten minutes. Don't overcook fish, or it will fall apart. Always add fish at the very end and reheat the broth gently, unless the recipe tells you to discard the fish altogether and enjoy only the taste it leaves behind.

Flounder and whiting break down as they simmer, but are useful in thickening most broths; halibut and cod add gelatin to the liquid that cooks them.

Any of the following fish can be used successfully in soups, chowders, and stews. If they have been frozen, thaw before cooking.

Bass (sea and freshwater)	Haddock
Cod	Hake
Cusk	Halibut
Flounder (sole)	Pollack
Grouper	Trout (sea and freshwater)
Goosefish (monkfish)	Whiting

In addition to these, crabs, lobsters, mussels, scallops, and clams also make delicious soup material.

HERBS

The flavors and colors that fresh herbs provide are far superior to their dried form. And once you start to season homemade soups, chowders, and stews with herbs grown in your own garden (or on a windowsill in winter), you'll wonder how you ever cooked without them.

Plant herbs in pots of rich soil (a mixture of compost, sand, topsoil, and manure), water diligently, and fertilize with blood meal or fish emulsion every two weeks.

Sink pots directly in the ground, or establish an herb garden and arrange them in clumps, rows, or designs. Many gardeners prefer to keep herbs in pots no matter how large their garden, for the convenience of moving them about.

To freeze herbs, chop fresh leaves or leaves and stems and spread them out on a baking sheet. (If leaves are small, keep whole.) Place in the freezer until brittle, spoon into plastic bags or jars, and return to the freezer. Although freezing maintains herb color and flavor better than drying, it is not practical to freeze all herbs.

To dry herbs, hang them by their stems or place in a hanging mesh basket designed to hold produce. Keep away from light and bottle when leaves are thoroughly dry. A faster method, but one that can spoil herbs if the temperature is too hot, is to place them on a baking sheet and bake in a slow oven (150°) with the door open until they are dry.

There are hundreds of different herbs to grow — each with its own requirements and uses in the kitchen. Here is a list of herbs that no cook should be without:

Basil. Treated as an annual in the North, basil reaches 18 inches in height and grows well from seed. Bush basil bears small clustered leaves; common basil has large broad leaves. Plants grow well from seed where planted in the spring, and thrive in a sunny but sheltered spot. If leaves begin to blanch, basil is getting too much sun. Continually pinch back the growing tips to keep plants bushy and don't let seed heads or flowers form.

Basil enhances the flavor of tomatoes, beef stew, carrots, spinach, peas, and potatoes. It is especially tasty with tomato soups, garlic, sage, summer savory, and in chicken, vegetable, and fish soups. Freeze basil, since it loses flavor and color when dried.

Chervil. One of the important herbs in French cooking, chervil's leafy vegetation looks like a cross between carrots and parsley. It performs as a perennial in protected gardens, growing as much as two feet high, and requires a sheltered or partially shaded area for best growth.

Sow in spring or fall in pots or directly in the garden by pressing seeds into fine soil and keeping them moist until germination occurs, in two to three weeks. Plant a large patch of chervil in your herb garden and cut it continually to encourage new growth. Don't let flowers form, and keep plants from drying out, since this will encourage them to bolt and flower quickly.

Use chervil in vegetable soups, and just about anywhere you'd use parsley, including as a garnish. Its flavor is readily lost through extended cooking, however, so add it minutes before serving. This is a difficult herb to preserve through freezing or drying. Keep a pot growing indoors for best results in winter.

Chives. One of the easiest and hardiest herbs to grow, chives last from year to year and seem to thrive on neglect. They adapt to almost any soil, but germinate slowly from seed. To start a clump, purchase a plant and water it well until established. The following year divide at the roots and space smaller divisions six to eight inches apart.

Chives have shallow roots and should be watered during extended dry periods. Fertilize if leaves begin to turn yellow. Don't let the purple, clover-like flowers form if you want a continual supply of greens. Cut all the way to the base when picking to encourage new growth.

An excellent garnish when chopped, chives impart a subtle onion flavor. They will grow indoors in a sunny window and they freeze well.

Dill. A member of the parsley family, dill is an annual that grows readily from seed where sown. It needs a constant supply of moisture to germinate and produce good foliage; during drought it bolts and goes to seed quickly. Sow dill in spring after danger of frost has passed. Harvest leaves before and after flower buds open. Dill is a good flavoring for soups that contain tomatoes, yogurt, sour cream, and potatoes, and in chicken soups and stews. In a sunny, protected place, it will often self seed. Dill does not freeze or dry well.

Lovage. This perennial herb has a celery-like taste and can be used in any soup where you want this flavor without the bulk of celery. Plant seeds in rich soil in full sun or partial shade. Divide mature plants in the fall or spring by separating eyes. Remove flower heads as they form to encourage bushy foliage. Lovage can reach three to four feet, and likes a constant supply of moisture. Use in pea, potato, and chicken soups. It will hold up for as long as an hour in simmering liquid. Use fresh or dried.

Marjoram. Of the three types of marjoram, sweet or knotted marjoram is the cook's herb. It adds a distinctive flavor to stocks, pork stews, and vegetable soups of all kinds. Treat it as an annual in the North or overwinter as a pot plant. It will grow 8 to 12 inches tall and prefers a sunny location. Cut stems when the plants flower, and dry or freeze the leaves.

Parsley. Parsley has appeared so often as a garnish color (and been pushed away as many times) that it is taken for granted as a decorative herb. The soup cook should get to know the flat-leafed variety, also known as Italian parsley, which has a strong peppery taste and adds flavor to any dish. It provides an edible bit of color

13

when diced and sprinkled atop cream soups, or soups lacking in accent.

Parsley likes moisture and should be planted in sun or partial shade. Seeds are slow to germinate, and should be soaked in warm water before sowing. Cut stalks to the base when harvesting to encourage new growth. Parsley will dry reasonably well but loses its flavor. Freeze for best results.

Rosemary. A slow-growing annual in the North, rosemary can be overwintered as a pot plant. For quickest results purchase a plant or two and transplant to a sheltered, well-drained soil. Propagate by cuttings in late summer. Use in vegetable soups and stocks, chicken and lamb stews. Pick leaves anytime to use fresh; take leaves for drying before the plant flowers.

Sage. Sage is a perennial with many different forms. The leafy, grayish-green sage is the most popular soup herb. Plant seedlings in rich soil and full sun and cut back each spring to encourage new growth and discourage woody development on older plants. Cut frequently to keep the plant bushy and harvest before flower spikes appear.

Sage sprawls to reach a height of two feet. Use in meat soups and stews. It dries slowly, and should not be hurried along in the oven. Don't let dry sage sit all winter in your kitchen, for it quickly loses its flavor.

Shallots. A relative of the onion, and not strictly an herb, the shallot does play an important role in seasoning soup. Although supermarkets occasionally stock paper packages of what they label as shallots, these can't compare to the plump, flavorful bulbs you can grow yourself.

Anything an onion can do a shallot can do better. Plant in spring or fall in rich, well-drained soil in a sunny location. Cut leaves and use in stocks and as a substitute for chives. The compound bulbs resemble garlic. (Shallots are available by mail from J.A. Demonchaux Co., 827 North Kansas Avenue, Topeka, KS 66608.)

Summer Savory. There are two savories, summer and winter. The former complements bean dishes, especially bean soups. Grow from seed in a sunny place. Mature plants reach two feet in height, but stems are sparse and the plant is one of the least decorative herbs. Harvest before flowers appear and dry for winter use. The flavor of summer savory holds up well in cooking.

Sweet Cicely. This perennial with delicate fern-like foliage is one of the earliest herbs to appear in the spring and it lasts well into the fall. It tolerates most soils and self seeds, reaching two to four feet at maturity. Press seeds into fine soil in spring or fall and keep moist until they germinate. Use in *bouquets garnis,* soups, and stews. Grow in partial shade, since leaves will blanch in strong sun. Sweet cicely does not dry well and is best used fresh.

Thyme. There are more than 100 species of thyme, in many habits and tastes. Perennial English and French thymes are the preferred choices for soup cookery to enhance meat stews, stocks, and dishes using wine. Thyme is also an important ingredient in *bouquets garnis.* Germination from seed is slow, so start with plants. Cut often to encourage foliage growth. Dry slowly in a dark place by harvesting leaf stalks when the first flowers open.

There are many ways to use herbs in soup-making. Whole sprigs of parsley, thyme, and marjoram can be added to stocks for flavor, and strained out after the proper cooking time has elapsed. Or, leaves of the most flavorful herbs can be chopped and incorporated into the broth, to float as bits of color and taste.

When making broths where you want the flavor of herbs but not their presence, bundle herbs together in such a way that they can be easily removed before the soup is served. Known as a *bouquet garni,* this can include several sprigs of fresh herbs bound together with thread at the stem ends, or combinations of fresh or dried herbs and spices tied up in a cheesecloth bag. A *bouquet garni* is added during the final simmering, and removed prior to serving.

Here are three basic suggestions for *bouquets garnis.* Experiment with what is available in your garden to create others.

BOUQUET GARNI WITH FRESH HERBS

3 sprigs parsley or 4 sprigs chervil	1 bay leaf 2 sprigs thyme

Cut herbs with stems as long as possible, and tie stems together with a piece of white thread.

BOUQUET GARNI WITH DRIED HERBS

2 tablespoons dried parsley
1 tablespoon dried thyme

1 bay leaf
1 tablespoon dried marjoram

Combine herbs and spoon into the center of two thicknesses of cheesecloth. Bring edges together, making a bundle, and tie off with string.

BOUQUET GARNI WITH HERBS AND SPICES

1 whole clove
1 blade mace

3 sprigs parsley
4 peppercorns

Combine herbs and spices and bundle as previously directed.

STORING

Soups can sit in the refrigerator for several days, vegetable soups generally keeping better than those containing meat. Most soups, including those with meat or poultry, can be frozen for as long as six months, but for better flavor, freeze just the stock and make soup from fresh ingredients.

Do not freeze soups or stews that contain rice, pasta, potatoes, or radishes. Pureed soups generally freeze well, unless they are made with raw vegetables. Pea soup is one of the best soups to freeze.

Reheat frozen soups in a heavy saucepan over low heat, or in a double boiler.

Chowders will keep in the refrigerator for up to two days but should be reheated each day. Because of the milk or cream and potatoes used in most recipes, chowders do not freeze well.

If you freeze a stew, use it in four to six weeks. For the best taste, cook only the meat and broth, cool, and freeze. When you're ready to serve the stew, reheat, cook vegetables separately and add when stew is heated through, along with ingredients such as rice or noodles.

COOKING EQUIPMENT

You need not invest in a kitchen full of gadgets to make good soups, chowders, and stews, but several items make the job easier:

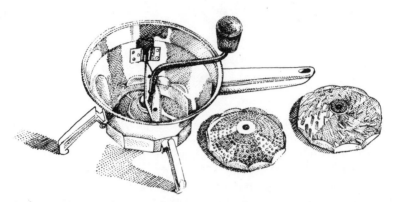

Food Mill. A device for pureeing and straining, the food mill comes in many shapes and sizes. The best for making a wide range of soups has interchangeable disks — coarse, medium, and fine — to do a variety of straining jobs. Many cooks prefer a food mill to a blender for all pureed soups, since it leaves a bit of texture in any mixture that goes through it.

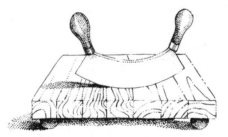

Mezzaluna. This half-moon chopper with two handles is used throughout Italy, and is available today all across the United States in gourmet supply stores. It does what a sharp knife can do, but makes the cutting more fun. It replaces the bowl and chopper once popular in New England kitchens.

17

Soup Kettle. The most important item for the soup cook is a good kettle. If you make a lot of soup, you might want to own several, in different sizes. One with an eight-quart capacity is the most practical, or you can go larger. Avoid thin aluminum kettles. Cast iron, enameled cast iron, and stainless steel are the best.

Dutch Oven. When making a stew, a Dutch oven or oven-proof casserole with a cover becomes an important piece of equipment. Enameled cast-iron casseroles come in many bright colors and with durable finishes.

Skillet. For sautéeing and frying, the cook needs a good pan. A heavy cast-iron skillet will last for years, but needs to be carefully maintained. New cast-iron pans should be washed and dried, then oiled several times to season them. Or rub with oil and set in a warm oven (250°) for half an hour. Never let a cast-iron pan dry in the open, or it will rust. To remove food particles stuck to the surface, sprinkle generously with salt and scour with a paper towel; repeat until clean. For tougher cleaning jobs, let skillet sit with water in it for a while, then pour off water, pour in salt, and rub. Enameled cast iron and stainless steel are ideal for all jobs.

Slotted (or perforated) Spoon. A simple implement, this will prove to be invaluable when skimming surface foam or fat, or when removing foods from liquid. Look for those made of plastic or stainless steel.

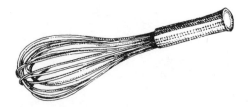

Whisk or Whip. These come in many sizes, with metal, wooden, or plastic handles. They work well for quick blending jobs and for slow stirring, especially of flour, milk, or cream.

Serving Bowls. The dish in which you serve a soup, chowder, or stew makes almost as much of an impression as its contents. Wide, shallow bowls are practical for serving most chunky chowders, stews, and soups. Chilled mixtures become elegant in glass cups or bowls. Traditionally, cream soup is served in a two-handled bowl; chowder in a heavy, oversized cup with one handle. Thin, hot soups can be served in mugs.

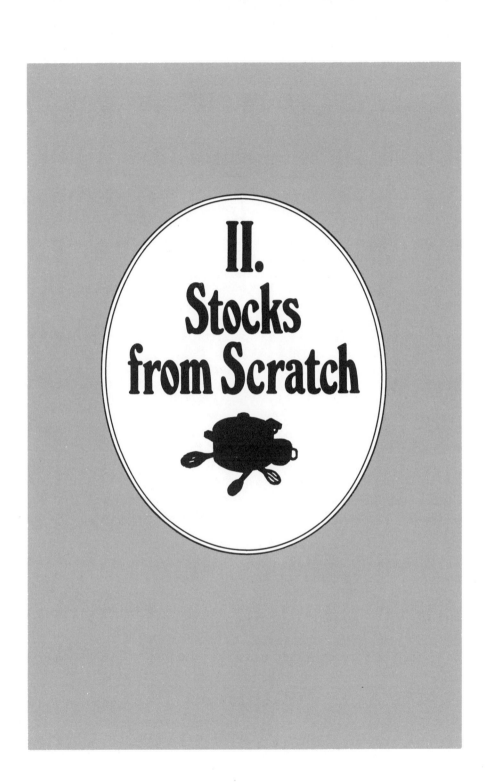

II.
Stocks
from Scratch

There is nothing difficult about making stock for soup; and once you get into the habit of cooking up a kettle full every week or so, as your eating habits require, you will find that you also use it in gravies and sauces.

In a pinch, use canned chicken or beef stock, or bottled clam juice, but these often leave a saltier taste in the final product and are less desirable than the delicately flavored stock you can make.

Use fresh ingredients — meat, bones, and vegetables. Vegetable and herb stocks make fine bases for vegetarian soups. Uncooked meat adds a rich taste and color to stock and is worth the cost. And nothing works as well as fowl (the toughest old bird your butcher has) for producing superb chicken flavor.

Throughout the years, cooks have extolled the virtues of adding vegetable scraps to stockpots; but some peelings are better suited to the compost pile since they give stock a bitter flavor and make it cloudy. Also, many store-bought vegetables are covered with a waxy coating which does not always scrub off completely; these parings shouldn't go into any stockpot.

Most vegetables can be used in stock, but avoid cabbage, cauliflower, and broccoli, which contribute bitterness. Carrots make stock sweet, tomatoes add acid. When using celery, include a good portion of leaves; the yellow ones have better flavor than older, green leaves. Onions need not be peeled when making stock, since their skins add a bit of color to the liquid they cook in.

As a general rule, use twice as much water as solids in your stock mixture, and start out with cold water — enough to cover the ingredients. Add a combination of meat, bones, and vegetables and bring to a boil. With a slotted spoon skim off the foam that collects on the surface, immediately reduce the heat, and simmer 30 minutes to several hours, depending on the kind of stock you are making: fish stock requires about 30 minutes; vegetable stock, one hour; chicken stock, two hours; and beef stock, three to four hours. Once you have reduced the heat under the stock, do not let it boil again.

Partially covered or uncovered stock becomes reduced in volume as it cooks, and turns into a more flavorful broth. Watch carefully so the liquid does not cook away completely.

When stock reaches the desired flavor, remove the kettle from the heat and cool at room temperature; transfer to a large bowl and chill, uncovered, in the refrigerator or in a cold back pantry. Skim the fat from the top and the stock is ready to use. To degrease it further, strain it through cheesecloth that has been soaked in hot water and wrung out, or drop ice cubes into warm stock and spoon out when fat collects on their surfaces.

CLARIFYING

The process of clarifying removes cloudy residue from cooked stock. For most soups, this step is not necessary, but it is suggested for any soup where a clear broth would enhance the overall appearance.

Before clarifying, taste the stock for flavor and adjust seasonings. Do not do this afterwards, or you may see additional clouding.

Skim fat from the top of chilled stock and place stock in a kettle or saucepan. For each pint of stock, you will need 1 beaten egg white and shell, and 2 teaspoons cold water. (The egg white acts as a magnet for the particles that make stock cloudy.) Beat egg white and cold water in a small bowl until foamy. Add to cold stock along with crushed egg shell. Slowly bring stock to a boil, stirring constantly. Boil 3 minutes, reduce heat, and simmer 20 minutes. Strain through cheesecloth, making sure the lowest point of the strainer does not come in contact with the strained stock.

Another method uses 2 egg whites for each quart of stock, but no shell. Beat whites in a bowl with 3 tablespoons cold broth. Add this mixture to remaining cold broth in a saucepan or kettle and blend with a whisk. Heat slowly to a boil, stirring constantly. Reduce heat and simmer 5 minutes. Pour hot stock through a strainer that has been chilled in the freezer.

STORING

If you do not use a homemade stock within 24 hours, it's best to freeze it — or, if you prefer to keep it in the refrigerator, be sure to reheat it just to a boil every second day.

For large amounts, measure and pour cooled stock into loaf pans, freeze until solid, then remove from pans by dipping them in hot water, just long enough for stock to come loose. Wrap blocks of stock in tinfoil or freezer paper and return them to the freezer. (Be sure to measure the stock before freezing so you know how many cupfuls are in each frozen block.)

If you have minimal freezer space, cook down the stock until it is condensed. Then pour it into ice cube trays, freeze, pack the cubes in plastic bags, and return to the freezer. One or two cubes will add extra flavor to many dishes.

HERB STOCK

3 to 4 stems and leaves of
   thyme, parsley, summer
   savory, basil, and chives

3½ cups cold water
1 potato, peeled and chopped
Salt to taste

Wash herbs and shake dry. Place in saucepan and mash with spoon. Add water, potato, and season with salt. Simmer, partially covered, 10 minutes. Remove from heat and let cool to room temperature. Strain. *Makes 4 cups.*

VEGETABLE STOCK

6 onions, sliced
½ cup chopped chives
3 stalks celery with leaves,
   chopped
3 carrots, peeled and chopped
¼ head cabbage, cored and
   sliced

3 sprigs parsley
1 bay leaf
3 leaves basil
2 sprigs thyme
2 quarts cold water

Combine all ingredients in soup kettle. Bring to a boil, reduce heat, and simmer, partially covered, 1 hour. Strain. *Makes 8 cups.*

BEEF STOCK I

1 pound beef, cubed
3 quarts cold water
2 teaspoons salt
1 carrot, peeled and chopped

1 red onion, chopped
1 stalk celery, chopped
4 sprigs parsley

Combine beef, water, and salt in soup kettle. Bring to a boil, add carrot, onion, celery, and parsley, reduce heat, and simmer, partially covered, 2½ hours. Skim several times during cooking. Strain broth, cool, and chill. Skim fat from top. *Makes 10 cups.*

BEEF STOCK II

4 pounds beef bones
  (preferably shin)
2½ quarts cold water
6 peppercorns
4 whole cloves
1 bay leaf

3 sprigs parsley
3 sprigs thyme
2 carrots, peeled and chopped
2 stalks celery, chopped
3 onions, chopped
Salt to taste

Place bones in soup kettle, add cold water and next 5 ingredients, and bring to a boil. Skim, reduce heat, and simmer, partially covered, 2 hours. Add vegetables and cook 1 hour longer. Strain through cheesecloth and cool. Skim fat from top. Season with salt.

Makes 8 cups.

BEEF STOCK III

6 pounds beef bones
  (preferably shin)
3 quarts cold water
6 peppercorns
6 whole cloves
1 bay leaf
2 sprigs thyme

1 sprig marjoram
2 sprigs parsley
2 carrots, peeled and chopped
2 stalks celery, chopped
1 turnip, peeled and chopped
1 onion, sliced
Salt to taste

Preheat oven to 350°. Place bones in roasting pan and cook 30 minutes. Remove bones to soup kettle, pour in juices and fat from pan, and add water. Bring to a boil, boil 5 minutes, and skim. Reduce heat and simmer 2 hours, partially covered. Add spices, herbs, and vegetables and cook 1 hour longer. Cool, strain, and chill. Remove fat from top. Season with salt.

Makes 10 cups.

VEAL STOCK

2 pounds veal knuckle bones
4 quarts cold water
Bouquet garni (see pages 15-16)
1 carrot, peeled and chopped

1 leek, chopped
1 stalk celery, chopped
2 onions, chopped

Preheat oven to 400°. Place bones in roasting pan and brown in oven 20 minutes. Remove meat, bones, and juices to soup kettle. Add remaining ingredients and simmer, partially covered, 3 hours. Skim occasionally. Strain. Cool, chill, and skim fat from top. *Makes 12 cups.*

25

LAMB STOCK

2 pounds lamb bones
2 quarts cold water
Dash of salt and pepper
1 bay leaf
2 sprigs thyme
6 peppercorns

1 potato, peeled and chopped
2 carrots, peeled and chopped
1 turnip, peeled and chopped
2 onions, chopped
3 stalks celery, chopped

Combine bones, water, and salt and pepper in soup kettle. Bring to a boil, skim, reduce heat, and simmer, partially covered, 2 hours. Remove bones. Cool broth, chill, and skim fat from top. Bring stock to a boil, add bay leaf, thyme, peppercorns, and vegetables; reduce heat, and simmer 1 hour, partially covered. Strain.   *Makes 6 cups.*

CHICKEN STOCK I

2 pounds chicken necks,
    wings, backs, etc.
2 quarts cold water
1 onion, sliced

2 stalks celery, sliced
1 sprig parsley
1 sprig thyme
8 peppercorns

Combine all ingredients in soup kettle. Bring to a boil, skim, reduce heat, and simmer 2 hours, partially covered. Strain, cool, and chill. Skim fat from top.   *Makes 6 cups.*

CHICKEN STOCK II

3-pound fowl
1 carrot, peeled and sliced
3 onions, sliced
1 bay leaf
2 sprigs lovage
4 sprigs parsley

3 leaves basil
1 sprig thyme
½ cup dry white wine
4 quarts cold water
Salt and pepper to taste

Combine all ingredients in soup kettle. Simmer, partially covered, 1½ to 2 hours. Skim occasionally. Strain through cheesecloth. Cool, chill, and skim fat from top.   *Makes 12 cups.*

TURKEY STOCK

1 turkey carcass (plus leftover
   bits of meat)
2½ quarts cold water
4 carrots, peeled and chopped
2 cloves garlic, chopped

2 teaspoons thyme or sage
¼ cup celery leaves
1 bay leaf
Salt and pepper to taste

Combine all ingredients in soup kettle. Simmer 2 hours, partially covered. Skim occasionally. Strain through cheesecloth. Cool, chill, and skim fat from top. *Makes 8 cups.*

CLAM STOCK

Use liquid from cooking clams as a base for chowder and fish soups. Place clams in soup kettle, add several inches of cold water and 2 sliced onions. Cover, bring to a boil, and steam until clam shells open. Remove clams with slotted spoon. Strain liquid through double layer of cheesecloth. If you need more stock than what remains from cooking the clams, stretch it by adding water, dry white wine, or bottled clam juice.

FISH STOCK

2 pounds fish frames,
   including 1 fish head
2 stalks celery, chopped
2 carrots, peeled and chopped
2 to 3 onions, chopped
1 clove garlic, coarsely
   chopped

1 cup chopped leek greens, or
   tops of 3 leeks
2 sprigs thyme
2 sprigs parsley
1 bay leaf
2½ quarts cold water

Combine all ingredients in soup kettle. Bring to a boil, skim, and simmer 30 minutes, uncovered. Strain. *Makes 10-12 cups.*

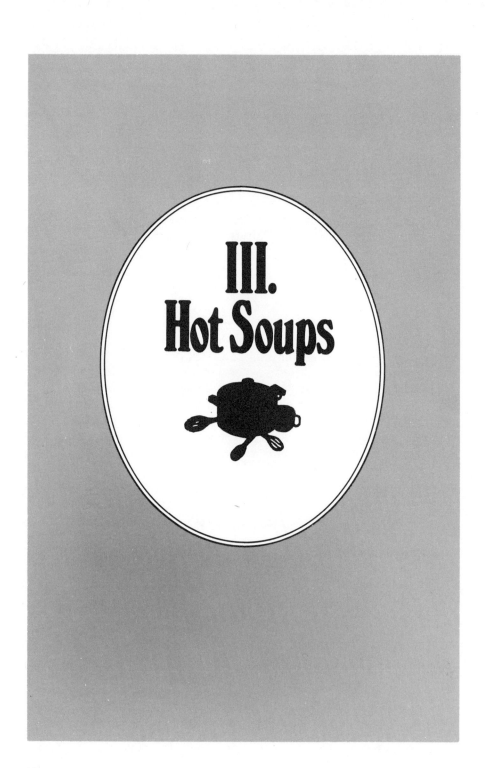

III.
Hot Soups

Consommés, Herb, and Nut Soups

CONSOMMÉ

Consommé is a rich broth that provides the cook with a versatile, clear soup. Serve hot or cold, and garnish as described below.

3 tablespoons butter	2 stalks celery, chopped
2½ pounds stew beef, cubed	1 onion, peeled and chopped
1 pound marrow bones	8 peppercorns
2 pounds beef knuckle	6 whole cloves
Cold water	2 sprigs thyme
4 cups beef stock	3 sprigs parsley
2 carrots, peeled and chopped	1 bay leaf

Melt butter in soup kettle. Cook stew beef over low heat, turning occasionally, until all sides are brown. Add bones and knuckle, cover with cold water, bring to a boil, and boil 5 minutes, skimming top. Reduce heat and simmer, uncovered, 2 hours. Skim occasionally. Add stock, vegetables, spices, and herbs. Cook 1 hour longer, adding more water as necessary. Strain, cool, and chill. Remove fat from top, clarify, reheat, and serve with desired garnish. *Serves 8-10.*

Garnishes for consommé: Choose any of the following or invent your own; there is no end to the possibilities. Consider color as well as flavor.

Thin strips of white chicken meat
Cooked baby peas
Matchstick slivers of carrots and/or zucchini
Chopped chervil, savory, rosemary, or chives
Cooked rice
Thinly sliced, sautéed mushrooms
Finely diced raw beets

HERB CONSOMMÉ

Try other combinations of fresh herbs to vary the flavor.

1½ quarts clarified chicken stock
2 tablespoons chopped chives
1 tablespoon chopped parsley

1 tablespoon chopped chervil
Salt and pepper to taste
Lemon slices
Chopped chervil

Heat stock to boiling in soup kettle and add herbs. Remove from heat and let herbs cook slowly as soup cools. After 15 minutes strain through cheesecloth and return broth to kettle. Season with salt and pepper, reheat, and serve hot. Garnish with thin slices of lemon and chopped chervil. *Serves 6.*

TOMATO CONSOMMÉ

Here's a good way to use up excess tomatoes from your garden.

3 to 4 large tomatoes, peeled and chopped
2 cups beef or chicken stock
1 teaspoon brown sugar

1 tablespoon chopped chervil
1 teaspoon vinegar
Salt and pepper to taste
Dill

Combine tomatoes, stock, and brown sugar in saucepan and simmer, partially covered, 30 minutes. Add chervil and cook 5 minutes longer. Press through food mill. Return to kettle, add vinegar, season with salt and pepper, and reheat. Garnish with fresh dill. *Serves 4.*

HERB SOUP I

Use whatever fresh herbs are available to make your own special blend.

3 tablespoons butter
1 head garden lettuce,
   shredded
1 small bunch watercress,
   chopped
1½ quarts chicken or herb
   stock

1 teaspoon chopped parsley
1 teaspoon chopped tarragon
Salt and pepper to taste
½ cup cream
1 egg yolk
Sliced radishes or chopped
   chives

Melt butter in saucepan. Sauté lettuce and watercress for 10 minutes.
Do not brown. Add stock and herbs and season with salt and
pepper. Cook 30 minutes, partially covered, over low heat. Remove
from heat. Cool slightly. Combine cream and egg yolk in separate
bowl. Pour ½ cup of hot soup into cream mixture, stir, and return
mixture to soup. Heat but do not boil. Garnish with thinly sliced
radishes or chopped chives. (Also good cold.)   *Serves 6-8.*

HERB SOUP II

Chicken stock may also be used as the base.

3 tablespoons butter
3 shallots, or 6 scallions
2 stalks celery with leaves,
   chopped
1 medium carrot, peeled and
   chopped

4 cups herb stock
1 egg yolk
½ cup cream
Salt and pepper to taste
Chopped summer savory or
   chives

Melt butter in soup kettle. Sauté shallots, celery, and carrot until
tender; do not brown. Add stock, bring mixture to a boil,
immediately reduce heat, and simmer gently 20 minutes, partially
covered. Press mixture through food mill. Return to kettle and
reheat. In small bowl beat together egg yolk and cream. Add ½ cup
hot soup liquid to egg mixture, blend with whisk, and pour back
into kettle. Reheat, stirring slowly, but do not boil. Season with salt
and pepper. Garnish with chopped summer savory or chives. (Also
good cold.)   *Serves 4.*

CHERVIL SOUP

Often substituted for parsley in French cooking, chervil is easy to grow and its taste is worth the extra space in your garden.

2 tablespoons butter
4 tablespoons chopped chervil
2 tablespoons flour

4 cups chicken stock
½ cup cream
Chopped chervil

Melt butter in skillet. Sauté chervil until tender. Sprinkle with flour and stir until smooth. Slowly add stock and heat, stirring until blended. Remove from heat and add cream. Reheat and serve garnished with additional bits of chopped chervil. *Serves 4.*

LOVAGE SOUP

Lovage is an easy-to-grow perennial herb that tastes like celery.

2 tablespoons butter
2 onions, peeled and sliced
3 tablespoons chopped lovage

1 tablespoon flour
3 cups chicken stock
1 cup milk or cream

Melt butter in saucepan. Sauté onions and lovage until tender. Sprinkle with flour and stir over low heat until blended. Slowly add stock and milk and stir until smooth. Simmer 5 minutes. Press through food mill and reheat. (Also good cold.) *Serves 4.*

ALMOND SOUP

Serve as a first course for a festive occasion.

2 cups slivered, toasted
   almonds
2 quarts chicken stock

2 egg yolks
2 cups cream

Combine almonds and stock in soup kettle. Bring to a boil, remove from heat, cover, and let stand 30 minutes. (If desired, puree mixture in food mill.) Reheat to a simmer. As stock is heating, beat together yolks and cream. Add ½ cup hot soup to egg and cream mixture, stir with a whisk until blended, and pour mixture into kettle. Heat thoroughly but do not boil. *Serves 8-10.*

CHESTNUT SOUP

Hot or cold, makes an elegant appetizer to a formal dinner. When fresh chestnuts are not available, use canned or dried.

1 pound chestnuts, peeled	½ cup milk
3 tablespoons butter	1 cup cream
5 cups chicken stock	2 egg yolks
Salt and pepper	Chopped parsley or paprika

To peel chestnuts, make an "x" on each round side, place in shallow pan, coat with vegetable oil, and bake at 400° until shells split — about 10 minutes. Peel off shells. Sauté peeled chestnuts in butter 5 minutes. Add 2 cups stock. Simmer, partially covered, 10 minutes or until nuts are soft. Cool and puree in blender. Combine pureed nuts with remaining 3 cups stock. Add salt and pepper to taste and simmer 5 minutes. Combine milk, cream, and egg yolks. Add ½ cup hot liquid to egg mixture, blend with whisk, and return mixture to soup. Heat gently and serve. Garnish with chopped parsley or paprika. *Serves 6-8.*

PEANUT SOUP

Use peanuts or peanut butter for this unusual soup.

3 tablespoons butter	¼ cup peanut butter or ½ cup
1 onion, peeled and chopped	roasted peanuts
1 tablespoon flour	½ cup cream
4 cups chicken stock	Dash of Tabasco

Melt butter in soup kettle. Sauté onion until tender. Sprinkle with flour and stir until blended. Add stock and heat to simmer, stirring constantly. Add peanut butter and stir until blended. (If peanuts are used, simmer mixture 15 minutes, covered, and puree in food mill.) Gently stir in cream and Tabasco and heat thoroughly. Do not boil.
Serves 4-6.

Dry Bean, Lentil, and Pea Soups

BAKED BEANS SOUP

Saturday night supper soup.

4 cups baked beans
Water

3 tablespoons catsup (or more
to taste)
Salt and pepper to taste

Combine beans with ½ cup water and puree in food mill or blender until smooth. Place in saucepan. Add additional water to desired consistency, along with catsup, and salt and pepper. Heat thoroughly.

Serves 4-6.

BEAN AND PORK SOUP

A stick-to-the-ribs soup for cold-weather appetites. Use beef stock instead of water for a richer broth.

2 cups dry navy beans
2 quarts cold water (less if
beans aren't drained)
1 pound spareribs, broken
into separate rib sections

3 onions, peeled and sliced
2 carrots, peeled and sliced
Salt and pepper to taste

Soak beans overnight in cold water. (Drain or not, as you prefer.) Combine beans, water, ribs, onions, and carrots in soup kettle. Bring to a boil, reduce heat, and simmer, partially covered, 1 hour or until beans are tender. Remove ribs, cut off bits of meat that remain, and return meat to kettle. Season with salt and pepper. Heat thoroughly.

Serves 6.

BLACK BEAN SOUP

Pass around a small pitcher of sherry and invite your guests to season their servings to taste.

2 cups dry black beans
1½ quarts cold water (less if beans aren't drained)
4 tablespoons oil
2 onions, peeled and chopped
2 stalks celery, chopped

3 cloves garlic, minced
1 teaspoon cumin powder
1 teaspoon oregano
Salt and pepper to taste
Lemon slices

Soak beans overnight in cold water to cover. (Drain or not, as you prefer.) Add beans to soup kettle with water, bring to a boil, reduce heat, and simmer, uncovered, 2 hours or until beans are tender. Add more water as necessary. Heat oil in skillet and sauté onions, celery, garlic, cumin, and oregano until tender. Add to beans and simmer 30 minutes. Press through food mill. Return to kettle, season with salt and pepper, and reheat slowly. Garnish with lemon slices.

Serves 6-8.

CRANBERRY BEAN SOUP

Cranberry beans are beige colored with red spots, and have a taste all their own. But if they are not available, substitute another variety of dry beans.

2 cups dry cranberry beans
1 cup whole dry peas
1 meaty ham bone
2 bay leaves
1 onion stuck with 4 cloves
3 quarts water (less if beans aren't drained)
5 potatoes, peeled and chopped

2 carrots, peeled and chopped
4 leeks, white parts only, chopped, or 3 onions, peeled and chopped
3 cloves garlic, minced
Grated Parmesan cheese

Soak beans and peas overnight in water to cover. (Drain or not, as you prefer.) Place in soup kettle with bone, bay leaves, and onion. Add enough water to make 3 quarts. Bring to a boil, reduce heat, cover, and simmer 2 hours or until beans are tender. Remove bone, chop meat into small bits, discard bone and return meat to kettle. Add potatoes, carrots, leeks, and garlic. Simmer, partially covered, 30 minutes or until vegetables are tender. Garnish with grated Parmesan cheese.

Serves 6-8.

HAM AND BEAN SOUP

Navy beans are preferred for this soup, but other varieties of dry beans can be used equally well.

2 cups dry navy beans	1 tablespoon chopped basil
2 quarts water (less if beans aren't drained)	1 onion, peeled and chopped
	4 peppercorns
1 meaty ham bone	2 stalks celery, sliced

Soak beans overnight in water. (Drain or not, as you prefer.) Combine beans, water, bone, basil, onion, and peppercorns in soup kettle. Cover and simmer 1½ hours. Add celery and simmer 30 minutes longer. Remove bone, cut off bits of meat, discard bone and add meat to soup. Heat thoroughly. *Serves 6-8.*

KIDNEY BEAN SOUP

Use a colorful garnish to contrast with the dark brown of the beans.

1 cup dry kidney beans	1 bay leaf
3 tablespoons butter	¼ teaspoon curry powder
3 onions, peeled and chopped	¼ teaspoon chili powder
2 cloves garlic, minced	Salt and pepper to taste
4 stalks celery with leaves, chopped	Sour cream
4 carrots, peeled and chopped	Chopped parsley
2 quarts beef stock (less if beans aren't drained)	

Soak beans overnight in cold water to cover. (Drain or not, as you prefer.) Melt butter in soup kettle, sauté onions, garlic, celery, and carrots until soft. Add stock, bay leaf, curry powder, chili powder, and beans. Simmer, uncovered, 2 hours or until beans are tender. Add more water as necessary. Press through food mill and return to kettle. Season with salt and pepper, reheat, and garnish with sour cream and chopped parsley. *Serves 8-10.*

LENTIL SOUP WITH HAM

Serve with warm, buttered corn bread or crisp taco chips.

2 cups dry lentils
2½ quarts cold water
1 meaty ham bone
3 tablespoons butter
2 onions, peeled and chopped
4 carrots, peeled and chopped

3 stalks celery, chopped
1 teaspoon cumin powder
½ teaspoon chili powder
2 teaspoons turmeric
Salt and pepper to taste
Chopped ham or parsley

Combine lentils and cold water in soup kettle. Add ham bone and simmer 1½ hours, partially covered. Stir occasionally. Add more liquid as necessary. As lentils finish cooking, melt butter in skillet. Sauté onions, carrots, and celery until barely tender. Add cumin, chili powder, and turmeric and stir until blended. Add vegetables to lentils. Simmer, partially covered, 30 minutes longer. Remove ham bone and set aside to cool. (If smooth soup is desired, press through food mill.) Cut meat from ham bone, chop, and add to soup. Heat slowly. Season with salt and pepper. Garnish with chopped ham or parsley. *Serves 8-10.*

LIMA BEAN AND SAUSAGE SOUP

Use large dry lima beans for this soup.

2 cups dry lima beans
½ pound bulk sausage meat
(or remove casings from
link sausage)

2 stalks celery, chopped
2 tablespoons flour
4 potatoes, peeled and sliced
Salt and pepper to taste

Soak beans overnight. (Drain or not, as you prefer.) Simmer in water to cover, 1½ hours, covered. As beans cook, fry sausage in skillet. Remove meat with slotted spoon and set aside. Leave 1 tablespoon fat in pan. Sauté celery in fat until tender. Sprinkle with flour and stir until blended. In separate pan boil potatoes in water to cover until tender. Drain. Slowly add ½ cup of hot bean liquid to flour mixture and stir until smooth. Add mixture to kettle along with potatoes and sausage. Heat thoroughly. Season with salt and pepper. *Serves 6-8.*

MEATLESS BEAN SOUP

This soup takes on different flavors depending upon what dry beans you use — navy, cranberry, pinto, etc.

2 cups dry beans
2 tablespoons butter
2 onions, peeled and chopped
3 cloves garlic, minced
2 stalks celery with leaves, chopped
2½ quarts cold water (less if beans aren't drained)

½ teaspoon chopped basil
1 carrot, peeled and sliced
3 tomatoes, peeled and chopped
1 pound green beans, cut in 1-inch pieces
Salt and pepper to taste

Soak beans overnight in cold water to cover. (Drain or not, as you prefer.) Melt butter in soup kettle. Sauté onions, garlic, and celery until soft. Add beans, water, basil, and carrot. Bring to a boil, reduce heat, and simmer, partially covered, 1 hour or until beans are tender. Add more water if necessary. Add tomatoes, green beans, and salt and pepper. Bring to a boil, reduce heat, and simmer 10 minutes, stirring occasionally, until green beans are tender.

Serves 8-10.

NAVY BEAN SOUP

Bean soups form the backbone of hearty New England fare. This is a simple soup but well-suited to entertaining.

2 cups dry navy beans
1 meaty ham bone
3 carrots, peeled and chopped

3 to 4 cloves garlic, minced
Salt and pepper to taste

Soak beans overnight in water to cover. (Or use the quick method: place in soup kettle with water to cover, bring to a boil, simmer, covered, 2 minutes; remove from heat and let sit, covered, 1 hour.) Drain or not, as you prefer. Add ham bone and enough water to cover beans by 1 inch. Simmer, covered, 2 hours. Add carrots and garlic during last 30 minutes of cooking. Remove bone, cool, cut meat from bone, chop, and return to kettle. Reheat and season with salt and pepper.

Serves 6-8.

PASTA E FAGIOLI

Popular in Italian communities and restaurants throughout New Eng...
this can be made with many different shapes of pasta.

2 cups dry white beans
¼ pound salt pork, diced
1 onion, peeled and chopped
2 cloves garlic, minced
1 potato, peeled and chopped
3 tablespoons oil
2 quarts cold water (less if
   beans aren't drained)

2 tomatoes, peeled and
   chopped, or 1 cup canned,
   drained
Salt and pepper to taste
1 cup uncooked elbow
   macaroni
Chopped parsley

Soak beans overnight in cold water. (Drain or not, as you prefer.) Fry salt pork in soup kettle until crisp. Remove with slotted spoon and set aside. Sauté onion and garlic in fat until tender. Add beans, potato, oil, water, tomatoes, and reserved salt pork. Cover and simmer 2 hours. Season with salt and pepper. Add macaroni and cook 5 to 10 minutes longer. Garnish with chopped parsley. *Serves 4-6.*

PORTUGUESE BEAN SOUP I

For a spicier soup, substitute 1 pound linguiça sausage for ham hock and add a half teaspoon cumin powder.

½ pound ham hock
2 bay leaves
1 tablespoon chopped basil
5 cups chicken stock
2 carrots, peeled and chopped
1 onion, peeled and sliced
¼ cup chopped cooked ham

¾ cup tomato juice
2 cups tomato sauce
4 cups kidney beans, canned,
   or dry, cooked
1 potato, sliced
⅓ head cabbage, shredded
Salt and pepper to taste

Combine hock with bay leaves, basil, and stock in soup kettle. Cover and simmer 1 hour or until meat separates from bone. Remove bone, cut off meat, and return meat to kettle. Add carrots, onion, ham, tomato juice and sauce and simmer, partially covered, 10 minutes or until vegetables are tender. Add beans, potato, and cabbage and cook 10 minutes longer or until vegetables are tender. Season with salt and pepper. *Serves 10-12.*

PORTUGUESE BEAN SOUP II

Almost any vegetable can be used here. Serve with corn bread.

2 cups dry kidney beans
3 tablespoons oil
2 green peppers, cored and
  chopped
4 stalks celery and leaves,
  chopped
4 scallions, chopped
1 pound linguiça sausage,
  sliced
4 hot Italian sausages, casings
  removed

3 cans (1 pound each)
  tomatoes
¼ cup red wine
1 bay leaf
1 can (6 ounces) tomato paste
1 cup chopped spinach or kale
2 to 3 potatoes, peeled and
  chopped
Salt and pepper to taste

Soak beans overnight in cold water to cover. (Drain or not, as you prefer.) Heat oil in skillet and sauté green peppers, celery, and scallions until tender. Remove with slotted spoon and set aside. Add sausages and fry until brown. Drain off fat. Combine all but last ingredients in soup kettle, add cold water to cover, and simmer, partially covered, 1½ to 2 hours. Season with salt and pepper.

Serves 8-10.

SPLIT PEA SOUP

Thick, nutritious, simple, and delicious.

2 cups green split peas
2½ quarts cold water
2 onions, peeled and chopped
1 stalk celery with leaves,
  chopped

1 meaty ham bone
1 cup cream
Salt and pepper to taste
Croutons

Combine split peas, water, onions, celery, and ham bone in soup kettle. Bring almost to a boil, reduce heat, and simmer gently, partially covered, 2½ hours. Remove bone and press mixture through food mill. Return to kettle, add cream, and heat slowly. Chop meat from ham bone and return to kettle. Season with salt and pepper. Garnish with croutons. *Serves 6-8.*

SPLIT PEA CURRY SOUP

Serve as a main course with English muffins.

1 cup yellow split peas
5 cups cold water
4 strips bacon, diced
1 small onion, peeled and
  chopped
1 clove garlic, minced
Salt and pepper to taste

1 cup canned whole tomatoes,
  crushed, with juice
2 stalks celery, chopped
2 carrots, peeled and chopped
2 tablespoons chopped
  parsley
½ to 1 teaspoon curry powder

Combine split peas, water, bacon, onion, garlic, salt and pepper in soup kettle and simmer, partially covered, 2 hours or until peas are tender. Add tomatoes, celery, carrots, parsley, and curry powder. Cook 15 minutes longer, or until vegetables are tender but still firm.

Serves 4-6.

SOPHIE'S SPLIT PEA SOUP

Madeira contributes a special flavor; add it right before serving.

2 cups split peas
2 quarts cold water
2 stalks celery, chopped
2 to 3 onions, peeled and
  chopped
2 carrots, peeled and chopped

1 bay leaf
2 sprigs thyme
4 knockwurst, sliced
Salt, pepper, and Madeira to
  taste
Croutons

Combine split peas and water in soup kettle. Bring to a boil, reduce heat, and simmer 2 minutes. Remove from heat and let stand 1 hour. Add vegetables, bay leaf, and thyme. Simmer, partially covered, 2½ hours or until peas are soft. Press mixture through food mill. Return to kettle. Add knockwurst and additional water if necessary. Simmer 30 minutes. Season with salt, pepper, and Madeira. Garnish with croutons.

Serves 6-8.

Vegetable Soups

CREAM OF ASPARAGUS SOUP

Fresh asparagus makes this impossible to resist, but frozen works almost as well.

2 pounds fresh asparagus, cut
    into ½-inch pieces
½ cup cold water
3 tablespoons butter

2 tablespoons flour
2 cups milk
1 cup cream
Salt and pepper to taste

Combine asparagus and water in saucepan, bring to a boil, reduce heat, cover, and simmer 5 minutes or until asparagus is just tender. Melt butter in soup kettle. Add flour and stir over low heat until blended. Slowly add milk and cream and blend with whisk until mixture is smooth. Add asparagus and cooking liquid, stir, and simmer 5 minutes. Season with salt and pepper. *Serves 4-6.*

BORSCHT

Equally good served cold — just press through a food mill and chill.

1 ham bone, or 1 pound beef
    bones
2½ quarts boiling water
½ head cabbage, shredded
2 onions, peeled and sliced
2 carrots, peeled and sliced
2 stalks celery, sliced
10 peppercorns
1 bay leaf

12 medium beets, peeled and
    diced or grated
2 tablespoons vinegar
1 teaspoon sugar
4 tomatoes, peeled and
    chopped
Salt and pepper (optional)
Yogurt or sour cream
Dill

Combine bones, water, cabbage, onions, carrots, celery, peppercorns, and bay leaf in soup kettle. Cover and simmer 45 minutes. In a saucepan mix beets with vinegar and sugar. Add water to cover. Simmer, partially covered, 15 minutes or until tender, and set aside. Add tomatoes to kettle and simmer 10 minutes. Strain stock, pressing juice from vegetables. Cool, chill, and skim off fat. Reheat to simmer. Add beets and cooking liquid and simmer 5 minutes. Season with salt and pepper, if desired. Garnish with yogurt or sour cream and dill.   *Serves 8-10.*

BROCCOLI-CHEESE SOUP

If broccoli isn't available, use cauliflower instead.

1 large bunch broccoli, chopped
2 tablespoons butter
2 shallots or 1 small onion, minced
1 clove garlic, minced

1 tablespoon flour
4 cups chicken stock
2 cups shredded sharp cheddar cheese
¼ cup sliced black olives
Salt and pepper (optional)

Boil or steam broccoli until tender. As broccoli cooks, melt butter in soup kettle. Sauté shallots and garlic until tender. Sprinkle with flour and stir over low heat until blended. Add stock and continue stirring until mixture is smooth. Add cheese and stir until melted and smooth. Add broccoli and olives and heat slowly. Season with salt and pepper, if desired.   *Serves 4-6.*

CREAM OF BRUSSELS SPROUTS SOUP

Trim the Brussels sprouts of any discolored outer leaves and cut an "x" in their bases before cooking. Boil or steam them whole until just tender.

4 tablespoons butter
2 shallots or scallions, chopped
3 tablespoons flour
½ cup milk
1 cup cream

5 cups chicken stock
5 cups Brussels sprouts, cooked and finely chopped
Salt and pepper to taste
Crumbled cooked bacon or chopped parsley

Melt butter in soup kettle. Sauté shallots until soft. Sprinkle in flour and stir until blended. Slowly add milk and cream and stir until smooth. Add stock and Brussels sprouts. Simmer 10 minutes, uncovered. Do not boil. Season with salt and pepper. Garnish with crumbled bacon or chopped parsley.   *Serves 4-6.*

CABBAGE SOUP

In winter, try sauerkraut in place of fresh cabbage.

1 head cabbage, shredded
4 to 5 cups water or beef stock
3 to 4 large potatoes, peeled
   and chopped
1 onion, peeled and chopped
4 tomatoes, peeled and
   chopped
4 carrots, peeled and chopped

1 turnip, peeled and chopped
1 stalk celery, chopped
2 parsnips, peeled and
   chopped
1 bay leaf
Salt and pepper to taste
Sour cream
Dill

Combine all but last 2 ingredients in large soup kettle and simmer 30 minutes, partially covered, or until vegetables are tender. Remove bay leaf. Serve in large bowls, and garnish with sour cream and dill.

Serves 8-10.

BREAD AND CABBAGE SOUP

Crusty French bread several days old holds up well in this soup. Don't use very soft bread or it will lose its shape entirely.

4 tablespoons butter
1 head cabbage, cored and
   chopped
1 loaf French bread, cut into
   2-inch-thick slices

1 cup grated Parmesan cheese
4 to 6 cups rich chicken stock

Preheat oven to 350°. Melt butter in Dutch oven. Toss cabbage in butter, cover, and cook over very low heat until cabbage is wilted. Remove most of the cabbage, leaving a layer about 2 inches deep. Cover with a layer of bread slices, sprinkle with cheese, and repeat layers, ending with cheese on top. Pour in enough stock to barely cover top layer. Bake 1 hour, uncovered, or until top is brown.

Serves 8-10.

CARROT SOUP

For a special treat, use tender baby carrots.

2 tablespoons butter
2 onions, peeled and chopped
2 tablespoons chopped
   parsley
2 teaspoons chopped sage

2 tablespoons flour
4 cups beef stock
8 carrots, peeled and chopped
Salt and pepper to taste

Melt butter in soup kettle. Sauté onions, parsley, and sage until tender. Sprinkle with flour and stir gently but quickly until well blended. Slowly add stock, stirring constantly until mixture is smooth. Add carrots and simmer, partially covered, over low heat for 20 minutes or until carrots are tender. (Baby carrots may require only 10 minutes.) Press through food mill, season with salt and pepper, and reheat — or chill and serve cold. *Serves 4-6.*

For Cream of Carrot Soup: Add ½ to 1 cup cream to pureed soup and reheat; also good cold.

CARROT AND PARSLEY SOUP

A colorful soup, flecked with orange and green.

2 carrots, peeled and grated	1 egg yolk
½ cup chopped parsley	½ cup cream
4 cups chicken stock	Chopped parsley

Combine carrots, parsley, and stock in soup kettle and simmer, partially covered, 20 minutes or until carrots are tender. Combine egg yolk and cream in small bowl. Pour ½ cup hot soup into egg mixture, blend with whisk, and return to soup. Garnish with chopped parsley. *Serves 4.*

CREAM CHEESE AND CARROT SOUP

Rich in flavor and nutrition.

4 tablespoons butter	1½ cups yogurt
3 carrots, peeled and chopped	1 cup milk
2 onions, peeled and chopped	2 egg yolks
3 tablespoons flour	Salt and pepper to taste
4 cups chicken stock	Chopped chives
16 ounces cream cheese, softened	

Melt butter in soup kettle and sauté carrots and onions until tender. Sprinkle with flour and stir until blended. Slowly add stock, stirring constantly until smooth. Bring to a boil, reduce heat, and simmer, partially covered, 10 minutes. Beat together cream cheese, yogurt, milk, and egg yolks. Remove soup from heat, cool 10 minutes, and stir in cheese and egg mixture. Reheat, stirring constantly until mixture is smooth. Do not boil. Season with salt and pepper. Garnish with chopped chives. *Serves 6-8.*

CAULIFLOWER SOUP

A light soup that makes a good appetizer. Served cold, it resembles vichyssoise.

1 large head cauliflower,
  chopped
2 quarts chicken stock
1 egg

1½ cups cream
Salt and pepper to taste
Chopped chives

Combine cauliflower and stock in soup kettle and simmer, partially covered, 20 minutes or until cauliflower is tender. Drain, reserving liquid, and set aside ½ cup cooked pieces. Press remaining cauliflower through food mill. Return to kettle with reserved liquid and simmer 5 minutes. In separate bowl combine egg with cream. Pour ½ cup hot soup liquid into egg mixture, blend with whisk, and return mixture to kettle. Heat thoroughly but do not boil. Spoon reserved cauliflower into soup bowls and pour hot soup over the pieces. Sprinkle with chopped chives. *Serves 6-8.*

CREAM OF CELERY SOUP

If you like the flavor of celery, you'll love this tasty soup!

2 tablespoons butter
1 onion, peeled and chopped
4 to 5 stalks celery, finely
  chopped
¼ cup chopped celery leaves

1 tablespoon flour
1 cup chicken stock
1 cup cream
Salt and pepper to taste

Melt butter in soup kettle or saucepan. Sauté onion, celery, and celery leaves until tender. Sprinkle with flour and stir until blended. Slowly add stock, stirring constantly until mixture is smooth. Add cream and cook 5 minutes over low heat until soup thickens. Season with salt and pepper. *Serves 4.*

DANDELION SOUP

New Englanders have long known the food value of dandelions, a green that nature provides in abundance in early spring. Harvest leaves when they have barely opened and are only a few inches high; large leaves are bitter and should not be used.

1 pound dandelion greens	1 cup cream
1 cup cold water	1 egg yolk
4 cups chicken stock	Croutons
1 teaspoon chopped basil	

Wash dandelion greens in warm water to remove dirt particles. Combine with cold water in soup kettle and simmer, covered, 10 minutes. Drain. Press through food mill and return to kettle. Add stock and basil and simmer 10 minutes. In separate bowl combine cream and egg yolk. Spoon ½ cup hot stock into cream mixture, blend with whisk, and return to kettle. Heat but do not boil. Garnish with croutons. (Also good cold.) *Serves 4-6.*

GRATED EGGPLANT SOUP

If members of your family don't like eggplant, this unusual soup may change their minds.

1 to 2 tablespoons oil	¼ teaspoon pepper
1 eggplant, peeled and grated	1 cup milk
1 onion, peeled and chopped	2 cups vegetable stock or
2 teaspoons chopped basil	vegetable cooking water
2 cloves garlic, minced	2 tablespoons soy sauce or
¼ cup butter	Tamari
¼ cup flour	¼ cup sherry

Heat oil in skillet and sauté eggplant, onion, basil, and garlic until tender; stir occasionally to prevent sticking. Melt butter in soup kettle, sprinkle with flour and pepper, and stir over low heat until blended. Slowly add milk, stirring until well blended and thickened. Add vegetable stock, soy sauce, and sherry. Stir in eggplant mixture, blending well. Heat thoroughly, but do not boil. *Serves 4.*

GARDEN SOUP I

Use up an abundance of vegetables from your garden with this soup. The choice of what to include is yours, but adjust cooking times when vegetables are added to keep them from overcooking.

2 quarts chicken or beef stock
1 teaspoon chopped basil
2 cloves garlic, chopped
5 peppercorns
1 bay leaf
1 cup green beans, cut into
   1-inch pieces

2 carrots, peeled and sliced
1 zucchini, sliced
2 tomatoes, peeled, seeded,
   and chopped
1 onion, peeled and chopped
Yogurt or sour cream

Pour stock into soup kettle. Tie basil, garlic, peppercorns, and bay leaf in cheesecloth and add to stock. Bring to a boil, reduce heat, and simmer 20 minutes, partially covered. Add beans and carrots, and simmer 10 minutes. Add zucchini, tomatoes, and onion, and simmer 10 minutes longer. Remove cheesecloth. Garnish with yogurt or sour cream. *Serves 6-8.*

GARDEN SOUP II

Fresh herbs and vegetables give this versatile soup the best possible flavor.

1 ham bone
¼ pound salt pork, diced
1 clove garlic, minced
3 sprigs parsley, chopped
2 carrots, peeled and diced
3 stalks celery, chopped
2 onions, peeled and chopped
1 cup fresh shell beans

4 large tomatoes, peeled and
   chopped
Few leaves each of mint,
   marjoram, basil, rosemary,
   and thyme
½ pound spinach, chopped
Salt and pepper to taste
Parmesan or Romano cheese

Cover ham bone with water in soup kettle and simmer, uncovered, 1 hour. Remove bone, skim off fat from broth. Cut meat from bone into bits and return to soup. Fry salt pork in skillet until crisp. Remove with slotted spoon and set aside. Add garlic, parsley, carrots, celery, and onions to fat and sauté until tender. Do not brown. Add sautéed vegetables to ham broth, along with beans, tomatoes, and herbs. Simmer, partially covered, 30 minutes. Add spinach and simmer 10 minutes longer. Season with salt and pepper and add reserved salt pork, if desired. Garnish with grated Parmesan or Romano cheese. *Serves 10-12.*

Substitutions: If fresh shell beans are not available, use ½ cup dry beans, soaked and cooked. Soldier beans, lentils, or chick-peas, or any combination of these works well. Add them to the soup with their cooking liquid, or drain and add with a small amount of water. Just about any other vegetable except beets, cabbage, or turnips can be added. Green peppers, summer squash, green or wax beans, peas, leeks, fennel or other herbs will add their own character and blend well with the ingredients called for above. If you don't have a ham bone, substitute beef bones or veal bones. For a vegetarian soup, omit the bone entirely.

GREEN BEAN SOUP

Use fresh green beans, but don't overcook them or they will lose their bright green color.

4 strips bacon
2 onions, peeled and chopped
1 clove garlic, minced
5 cups chicken or veal stock
1 bay leaf
3 tablespoons vinegar or
  lemon juice (optional)

2 potatoes, peeled and
  chopped
1 pound green beans, cut into
  1-inch pieces
Salt and pepper to taste

Fry bacon in soup kettle until crisp. Remove, drain, and set aside. Sauté onions and garlic in remaining fat until soft. Add stock, bay leaf, vinegar, and potatoes; bring to a boil, reduce heat, and simmer, partially covered, 15 minutes. Add beans and simmer 10 minutes longer or until beans are tender. Season with salt and pepper. Remove bay leaf. Garnish with reserved bacon, crumbled. *Serves 4-6.*

HALLELUJA SOUP

A traditional New England soup that is easy to make and sure to please.

½ pound salt pork, diced
3 onions, peeled and sliced
3 potatoes, peeled and sliced
2 carrots, peeled and sliced
4 cups chicken stock
1 tablespoon flour

½ cup dry white wine
2 leaves sage, minced
2 sprigs thyme
Salt and pepper to taste
Minced sage

Fry salt pork in soup kettle until crisp. Remove with slotted spoon and set aside. Sauté onions in fat until tender. Add potatoes and carrots, pour in stock, and simmer, covered, 20 minutes or until vegetables are tender. In small bowl blend flour, wine, and herbs. Stir until smooth. Pour ½ cup hot soup liquid into flour mixture, blend with whisk, and return mixture to soup kettle. Season with salt and pepper. Heat and serve garnished with minced sage or reserved salt pork. *Serves 4-6.*

CREAM OF JERUSALEM ARTICHOKE SOUP

Jerusalem artichokes are easy to grow; in fact, they can spread vigorously in an untended garden.

4 Jerusalem artichokes, peeled
   and coarsely chopped
1 onion, peeled and chopped
2 carrots, peeled and chopped
4 cups chicken stock

1 cup cream
2 egg yolks, beaten
2 tablespoons sherry
Salt and pepper to taste

Combine artichokes, onion, carrots, and stock in soup kettle, and simmer, partially covered, 10 minutes or until artichokes are soft. Press through food mill. Return to kettle. In separate bowl combine cream and egg yolks. Pour ½ cup hot pureed soup into egg and cream mixture, blend with whisk, and return mixture to kettle. Add sherry, heat, and season with salt and pepper. *Serves 4-6.*

KALE SOUP

Kale is a popular soup ingredient with Portuguese cooks from Gloucester to New Bedford and Provincetown. If unavailable, substitute spinach.

2 potatoes, peeled and cubed
1½ quarts cold water
½ pound chorizo or linguiça
   sausage, sliced

4 cups finely shredded kale (as
   thin as you can cut it)
Salt and pepper to taste

Combine potatoes and water in soup kettle and simmer, partially covered, 15 minutes or until tender. Meanwhile, sauté sausage in heavy skillet over low heat until brown. When potatoes are tender, mash in kettle with remaining water. Drain sausage and add to kettle with kale. Cover and simmer 10 minutes. Season with salt and pepper.   *Serves 4-6.*

LETTUCE SOUP

Lettuce performs surprisingly well in soup. Use Boston lettuce or another leaf lettuce (not iceberg), and cook over very low heat until shreds have broken down in the broth. For a rich soup cut stock back to 3 cups and add 1 cup cream at the end of cooking time.

2 heads Boston lettuce, cored
   and finely shredded
4 cups chicken or veal stock

Salt and pepper to taste
Croutons

Combine lettuce with 1 cup stock in soup kettle. Cover and simmer over very low heat 15 minutes. Add another cup of stock and simmer 15 minutes longer. Repeat with remaining stock, cooking up to 1 hour, until mixture is smooth. Garnish with croutons.   *Serves 4.*

CREAM OF MUSHROOM SOUP

A sprinkling of herbs or paprika will brighten up this creamy soup.

½ pound mushrooms, thinly
   sliced
1 onion, peeled and chopped
1 small stalk celery, chopped
2 cups water or chicken stock
4 tablespoons butter

2 tablespoons flour
1 quart milk, scalded
2 teaspoons Worcestershire
   sauce
Salt and pepper to taste
Chopped parsley or paprika

Combine mushrooms, onion, celery, water, and 2 tablespoons butter in soup kettle; simmer, partially covered, 15 minutes. In a saucepan melt remaining 2 tablespoons butter. Add flour and stir with whisk over low heat until smooth. Slowly add hot milk. Cook over low heat, stirring, until mixture is smooth and thickened. Pour into soup kettle. Add Worcestershire sauce and season with salt and pepper. Garnish with chopped parsley or paprika.   *Serves 4.*

MUSHROOM-ONION SOUP

Just as good with as without the cream.

2 tablespoons butter
2 cups sliced mushrooms
2 onions, peeled and chopped
½ cup dry white wine
1 bay leaf

2½ quarts chicken stock
1 cup cream
Salt and pepper to taste
Chopped parsley

Heat butter in soup kettle and sauté mushrooms and onions until tender. Pour in wine, add bay leaf, and simmer, uncovered, until liquid has almost evaporated. Add stock and heat. Stir in cream, season with salt and pepper, and heat again. Remove bay leaf. Garnish with chopped parsley.   *Serves 8-10.*

MUSHROOM AND POTATO SOUP

This will take the chill off any winter's day.

2 tablespoons butter
½ pound mushrooms,
   chopped
1 onion, peeled and chopped
2 tablespoons flour
5 cups chicken stock
2 potatoes, peeled and
   chopped

2 teaspoons Worcestershire
   sauce
1 tablespoon lemon juice
Salt and pepper to taste
Chopped chives

Melt butter in soup kettle. Sauté mushrooms and onion until tender. Sprinkle in flour and stir until blended. Slowly add stock, stirring until mixture thickens. Add potatoes, Worcestershire sauce, and lemon juice and simmer, partially covered, 20 minutes or until potatoes are tender. Season with salt and pepper to taste. Garnish with chopped chives.   *Serves 4-6.*

ONION SOUP

Slow cooking produces a rich onion flavor; the sugar colors onions and broth brown.

4 tablespoons butter
2 tablespoons oil
12 yellow onions, peeled and
  sliced
1 teaspoon sugar

4 tablespoons flour
2½ quarts boiling beef stock
Salt and pepper to taste
Parmesan or Swiss cheese

Melt butter in soup kettle. Add oil, stir in onions, and cook, covered, over low heat 20 minutes. Remove cover, increase heat slightly, sprinkle onions with sugar, and cook, stirring frequently, 20 minutes longer. Sprinkle onions with flour, stir until smooth. Gradually add hot stock, stirring constantly until smooth. Simmer, partially covered, 20 minutes. Garnish with grated Parmesan or baked cheese.   *Serves 8-10.*

To garnish with baked cheese: Preheat oven to 350°, pour hot soup into oven-proof bowls, and set on baking sheet. Place a round of toasted French bread on top of each bowl and sprinkle with a thick layer of grated Swiss cheese, or a mixture of Swiss and Parmesan. Dot cheese with butter and bake 15 minutes. If desired, after baking, run bowls under broiler for 1 or 2 minutes to brown cheese.

SWEET AND SOUR ONION SOUP

Red onions have the best flavor for this soup, but yellow onions will also work.

6 red onions, peeled and sliced
4 tablespoons butter
3 teaspoons sugar
2½ quarts chicken stock

3 teaspoons cinnamon
Juice of 2 lemons
Salt and pepper to taste
Cinnamon

Place onions in soup kettle and cover with cold water. Bring to a boil, reduce heat, and simmer, partially covered, 10 minutes. Drain. Melt butter in heavy skillet and sauté onions 10 minutes. Sprinkle with sugar and simmer, partially covered, 45 minutes. Press onions with chicken stock through food mill and return to kettle. Add cinnamon and lemon juice. Season with salt and pepper. Heat thoroughly. Garnish with a sprinkling of cinnamon.   *Serves 6.*

CREAM OF PEA SOUP

This "sweet" pea soup is a beautiful bright green. Try it with tender peas fresh from the garden.

4 cups fresh or frozen peas	1 teaspoon salt
2 cups water or chicken stock	¼ teaspoon pepper
1 cup cream	1 tablespoon butter
1 cup milk	Mint leaves
1 tablespoon flour	

Cook peas in water until tender. Press peas and liquid through food mill. Set aside. Combine cream and milk, scald, and remove from heat. Add flour and blend with whisk. Cook, stirring over low heat, until mixture thickens. Add salt and pepper, stir in pureed peas, and add butter. Serve hot, garnished with fresh mint leaves.   *Serves 4.*

PEA POD SOUP

Use pods of the much-acclaimed All-American Sugar Snap Peas to make this soup. Remove strings on pods before cooking.

4 cups tender pea pods	2 cups cream
4 cups chicken stock	2 tablespoons chopped chervil
2 yellow onions, peeled and chopped	Salt and pepper to taste
2 carrots, peeled and chopped	Chopped chervil

Combine pea pods, stock, onions, and carrots in soup kettle. Bring to a boil, reduce heat, cover, and simmer 30 minutes. Press through food mill. Return to kettle. Add cream and chervil and heat. Season with salt and pepper. Garnish with chopped chervil.   *Serves 4-6.*

LEEK AND POTATO SOUP

Leeks impart a delicate flavor and wonderful aroma, but if you can't find them, substitute onions.

2 tablespoons butter	Salt and pepper to taste
6 to 8 leeks, white parts only, sliced	3 to 4 potatoes, peeled and chopped
2 tablespoons flour	⅓ cup sour cream
4 cups hot water	Chopped chives

Melt butter in heavy skillet. Sauté leeks until tender. Do not brown. Remove pan from heat. Sprinkle flour over leeks and return pan to low heat. Cook several minutes, stirring constantly, until flour is well blended. Remove from heat. Add hot water, ½ cup at a time, stirring constantly until blended. Season with salt and pepper. Heat to simmer, add potatoes, and cook, partially covered, 20 minutes or until potatoes are tender. Stir in sour cream and serve, or press mixture through food mill. Garnish with finely chopped chives. *Serves 4.*

MASHED POTATO SOUP

A fine way to make use of a small dab of leftovers.

2 tablespoons butter	2 cups cream
2 carrots, peeled and chopped	1 cup mashed potatoes
1 stalk celery, chopped	Salt and pepper to taste
1 onion, peeled and chopped	Chopped parsley

Melt butter in saucepan and sauté carrots, celery, and onion until tender. Add cream and heat almost to a boil. (Do not boil.) Add potatoes and stir until blended. Season with salt and pepper. Garnish with chopped parsley. *Serves 4.*

POTATO SOUP

Smooth and satisfying.

4 potatoes, peeled and chopped	1 onion, peeled and chopped
2 cups chicken stock	2 tablespoons flour
4 tablespoons butter	1 quart milk, scalded
1 stalk celery, chopped	Salt and pepper to taste
	Parsley

Combine potatoes and stock in soup kettle. Simmer, covered, 15 minutes or until tender. As potatoes cook, melt butter in skillet. Sauté celery and onion until soft. Sprinkle with flour and stir until blended. Add to kettle and stir. Press potatoes, stock, celery, and onion through food mill. Return mixture to kettle. Slowly add hot milk, stirring until smooth. Season with salt and pepper. Garnish with parsley. *Serves 6-8.*

POTATO AND BARLEY SOUP

A good winter soup.

2 tablespoons butter
1 cup sliced mushrooms
1 onion, peeled and chopped
¼ cup barley
3 carrots, peeled and chopped
1½ quarts beef stock

3 potatoes, peeled and
  chopped
1 cup cream
Salt and pepper to taste
Dill

Melt butter in soup kettle and sauté mushrooms and onion until tender. Add barley, carrots, and stock; bring to a boil, reduce heat and simmer, partially covered, 15 minutes. Add potatoes and cook 15 minutes longer or until tender. Stir in cream. Heat thoroughly, but do not boil. Season with salt and pepper. Garnish with dill.

Serves 6-8.

POTATO AND WATERCRESS SOUP

Serve this inexpensive soup as a light lunch, or as an appetizer for a multi-course dinner.

4 to 5 potatoes, peeled and
  chopped
4 cups cold water
1 bunch watercress

1 tablespoon butter
½ cup milk
Salt and pepper to taste

Combine potatoes and water in soup kettle. Boil 20 minutes or until tender. Drain and save water. Press potatoes through food mill and return to kettle with water. Chop watercress (reserving a few whole leaves for garnish), add to kettle, and cook 5 minutes. Add butter and milk. Heat until warm, season with salt and pepper, and garnish with watercress leaves. (Also good cold.) *Serves 4-6.*

SCOTCH POTATO SOUP

For a smooth, cold soup, press through a food mill and chill before serving.

6 tablespoons butter
4 to 5 leeks, white and half of
  green parts, sliced
2 stalks celery, chopped
1½ quarts milk
3 to 4 potatoes, peeled and
  diced

2 tablespoons flour
1 teaspoon salt
½ teaspoon pepper
Crumbled bacon or chopped
  parsley

Melt 4 tablespoons butter in heavy skillet. Sauté leeks and celery until tender. Scald milk in soup kettle and stir in leeks and celery. Simmer, uncovered, over very low heat 30 minutes. In a separate pan cook potatoes in boiling water 10 minutes and drain. Put remaining 2 tablespoons butter in a saucepan and slowly stir in flour until mixture is smooth. Add ½ cup liquid from soup kettle and stir until thickened. Return mixture to kettle. Add potatoes to kettle, cover, and simmer 15 minutes. Season with salt and pepper. Garnish with bacon or chopped parsley.   *Serves 6-8.*

PUMPKIN SOUP

Instead of the usual baked or steamed pumpkin for the holidays, serve it as soup.

1 tablespoon butter
1 small onion, peeled and
  minced
1 pound fresh pumpkin,
  steamed, drained, and
  pureed, or 1 can (14½
  ounces)

2 cups chicken stock
½ teaspoon thyme
1 bay leaf
1 cup cream
¼ cup dry sherry
Chopped parsley or chives

Melt butter in soup kettle. Sauté onion until golden. Stir in pumpkin, stock, thyme, and bay leaf. Cook over low heat 15 minutes, stirring occasionally, until mixture is smooth. Remove from heat and cool. Stir in cream and sherry and heat thoroughly. Remove bay leaf. Garnish with chopped parsley or chives.   *Serves 4-6.*

SALSIFY SOUP

Salsify, also known as "oyster plant" for its oyster-like flavor, grows like carrots and parsnips.

10 to 12 salsify roots	1 tablespoon flour
4 cups cold water	2 cups milk
1 bay leaf	1 teaspoon salt
1 onion, peeled and chopped	¼ teaspoon white pepper
1 tablespoon butter	

Peel salsify roots and immediately place in pan of cold water to cover. Pour 4 cups cold water into soup kettle. Slice roots thinly, one at a time, and add to kettle. Add bay leaf and onion. Simmer, partially covered, 30 minutes. Melt butter in small saucepan. Over low heat, blend in flour with whisk, stirring, and pour in milk. Stir until mixture is smooth. Add to kettle along with salt and pepper. Stir until smooth and heat thoroughly.   *Serves 4.*

For Cream of Salsify Soup: Grate salsify before cooking and proceed as above. Beat together ¼ cup cream and yolk of 1 egg, and add to soup at end of cooking time.

SAUERKRAUT SOUP

Sauerkraut makes a delicious soup to serve with sausages or roast meat, or as a complete meal in itself.

3 tablespoons butter	3 cups sauerkraut
2 onions, peeled and sliced	2 tablespoons chopped
2 tablespoons flour	parsley
¼ cup tomato puree	Salt and pepper to taste
5 cups beef stock	Chopped parsley

Melt butter in soup kettle. Sauté onions until tender. Sprinkle with flour, and stir in tomato puree until mixture is smooth. Add stock, sauerkraut, and parsley. Bring to a boil, reduce heat, cover, and simmer 30 minutes. Season with salt and pepper. Garnish with additional chopped parsley.   *Serves 4-6.*

SCALLION SOUP

Use both white and green portions of the scallions.

3 tablespoons butter	½ cup finely chopped spinach
6 scallions, sliced	1 tablespoon chopped basil
3 carrots, peeled and grated	2 teaspoons chopped parsley
4 cups chicken stock	Salt and pepper to taste

Melt butter in soup kettle and sauté scallions until soft. Add carrots, stock, spinach, basil, and parsley; bring to a boil, reduce heat and simmer, uncovered, 10 minutes. Season with salt and pepper.

Serves 4-6.

SPINACH SOUP I

Pass around a bowl of grated Parmesan cheese to sprinkle on top.

1 pound fresh spinach	1 stalk celery, sliced
1 carrot, peeled and sliced	4 cups chicken stock
1 onion, peeled and sliced	Croutons

Wash spinach in warm water. Place in soup kettle with carrot, onion, celery, and stock. Simmer, partially covered, 20 minutes. Press through food mill. Return to kettle and reheat. Garnish with croutons. *Serves 4.*

SPINACH SOUP II

Wash spinach in warm, not cold, water to remove the dirt that clings to the leaves.

3 tablespoons butter	4 cups chicken or vegetable
1 carrot, peeled and chopped	stock
1 pound fresh spinach, chopped, or 1 package frozen chopped spinach, thawed	2 tablespoons chopped parsley
	2 tablespoons lemon juice
1 onion, peeled and chopped	Salt and pepper to taste
2 tablespoons flour	Croutons

Melt butter in soup kettle. Sauté carrot, spinach, and onion until soft. Sprinkle in flour and stir over low heat until blended. Slowly add stock, stirring until smooth. Heat to a boil, reduce heat, add parsley and simmer, uncovered, 5 minutes. Press mixture through food mill. Add lemon juice and heat thoroughly. Season with salt and pepper. Garnish with croutons. *Serves 4-6.*

RICH CREAM OF SPINACH SOUP

Appealing even to those who think they don't like spinach.

4 tablespoons butter
¼ cup minced yellow onions
3½ cups shredded spinach
  (packed)
2 tablespoons flour
1½ quarts boiling chicken or
  veal stock

3 egg yolks
½ cup cream
1 to 3 tablespoons butter
  (optional)
Diced sweet red pepper or
  chopped parsley

Melt 4 tablespoons butter in saucepan and sauté onions until tender. Add spinach and cook over low heat 5 minutes. Sprinkle with flour and stir over low heat until blended. Remove pan from heat and beat in stock, 1 cup at a time. Simmer, covered, 10 minutes. In bowl combine egg yolks and cream. Add ½ cup of hot stock to egg mixture, blend with whisk, and return mixture to soup. Reheat over low heat, stirring gently; do not boil. Remove from heat. If desired, stir in 1 to 3 tablespoons butter. Garnish with diced sweet red pepper or finely chopped parsley.   *Serves 4-6.*

SPINACH AND TOMATO SOUP

For a smooth soup, puree before serving.

1 pound fresh spinach,
  chopped and cooked
5 cups beef, chicken, or
  vegetable stock
1 cup tomato puree

1 carrot, peeled and chopped
1 potato, peeled and chopped
1 tablespoon lemon juice
Salt and pepper to taste
Sour cream

Combine spinach, stock, tomato puree, carrot, and potato in soup kettle. Bring to a boil, reduce heat, and simmer, partially covered, 20 minutes or until vegetables are tender. Add lemon juice and season with salt and pepper. Garnish with sour cream.   *Serves 4-6.*

SPRING SOUP

Here's a soup to serve in celebration of winter's end.

4 tablespoons butter
½ pound spinach, chopped
½ pound watercress, chopped
3 tablespoons chopped chervil
2 tablespoons flour

4 cups chicken stock
1 egg yolk
1 cup cream
Salt and pepper to taste

Melt butter in soup kettle. Add spinach, watercress, and chervil and sauté over low heat until wilted, about 5 minutes. Sprinkle with flour and stir until blended. Add stock and simmer 10 minutes, stirring until smooth. Press mixture through food mill. Return to kettle and heat. In separate bowl combine egg yolk and cream. Add ½ cup hot liquid to egg mixture, blend with whisk, and return to kettle. Stir until blended. Season with salt and pepper.   *Serves 4.*

TOMATO SOUP

Fresh parsley complements this tasty, light red soup.

4 cups beef stock
1 bay leaf
6 cups fresh tomatoes, peeled
    and chopped, or canned,
    undrained and chopped
2 tablespoons chopped
    summer savory
1 clove garlic, minced

2 onions, peeled and chopped
4 carrots, peeled and sliced
2 stalks celery, chopped
½ cup chopped parsley
1 potato, peeled and chopped
Salt and pepper to taste
Chopped parsley

Combine all but last 2 ingredients in soup kettle. Heat just to a boil, reduce heat, and simmer, partially covered, 15 minutes or until vegetables are tender. Remove bay leaf. Press through food mill and season with salt and pepper. Garnish with chopped parsley.
Serves 4-6.

TOMATO-DILL SOUP

Serve as a first course, either hot or cold.

6 large, ripe tomatoes, peeled,
    cored, and chopped
1 onion, peeled and chopped
½ teaspoon celery seed

3 sprigs dill
1½ cups chicken stock
1 cup sour cream
Sliced tomato or chopped dill

Combine tomatoes, onion, celery seed, dill, and stock in soup kettle and simmer, partially covered, 15 minutes. Press mixture through food mill. Cool slightly. Add sour cream and heat slightly — or chill. Garnish with thin slices of tomato or chopped dill.   *Serves 4.*

TOMATO-EGGPLANT SOUP

Use small, tender eggplants for the best flavor.

3 small or 1 large eggplant
4 tablespoons butter
6 tomatoes, peeled, seeded,
   and chopped
2 onions, peeled and chopped
2 cloves garlic, minced

1 bay leaf
½ cup uncooked rice
2 quarts beef stock
Salt and pepper to taste
Chopped chives

Peel and cube eggplant. Soak 15 minutes in salted water and drain well. Heat butter in soup kettle, add eggplant, stir, cover, and cook 20 minutes over very low heat. Stir several times as eggplant cooks. Add tomatoes, onions, garlic, and bay leaf. Cover again and cook 10 minutes, stirring occasionally until vegetables are well blended. Add rice and stock. Cover and simmer 30 minutes. Season with salt and pepper. Garnish with chopped chives. *Serves 6-8.*

TOMATO AND HERB SOUP

You will always be ready for unexpected company with this spur-of-the-moment soup.

2 quarts tomato juice or V-8
   juice
Juice of 1 lemon
2 cloves garlic, crushed
1 teaspoon dry mustard
1 tablespoon chopped
   rosemary

1 tablespoon chopped basil
1 sprig thyme
Salt and pepper to taste
Chopped basil or sliced
   cucumber

Combine all ingredients except garnish and simmer, covered, 20 minutes. Strain, and garnish with chopped basil or thinly sliced cucumber. (Also good cold.) *Serves 6-8.*

TOMATO-NOODLE SOUP

Noodles add substance to this spicy soup, but it's also good without them.

2 tablespoons butter
1 onion, peeled and diced
1 clove garlic, minced
½ green pepper, cored and
  chopped

1 can (6 ounces) tomato paste
5 cups chicken stock
½ teaspoon dried oregano
Tabasco to taste
1 cup uncooked thin noodles

Melt butter in soup kettle. Sauté onion, garlic, and green pepper until soft. Stir in remaining ingredients except noodles and simmer 10 minutes. Bring to a boil, add noodles, and simmer until tender.

Serves 4-6.

TOMATO AND SWEET PEPPER SOUP

Flavors meld as this soup sits, and it tastes even better the second day.

3 tablespoons oil
3 onions, peeled and sliced
3 to 4 green peppers, cored
  and chopped
2 stalks celery, diced
1½ pounds tomatoes, peeled
  and chopped, or 3 cups
  (28-ounce can), drained

Salt and pepper to taste
7 cups boiling water
Grated rind and juice of 1
  lemon
Yogurt
Chopped dill, parsley, or
  chives

Heat oil in soup kettle. Sauté onions until soft. Add green peppers, celery, tomatoes, and salt and pepper, and cook over moderate heat 30 minutes. Add boiling water and increase heat. Cook 5 minutes. Add lemon rind and juice. Cool slightly. Press through food mill, reheat, and serve garnished with yogurt and chopped dill, parsley, or chives. (Also good cold.)

Serves 10-12.

TURNIP SOUP

Serve hot or cold, anytime when turnips are in season.

½ white turnip, peeled and
   chopped
1 carrot, peeled and chopped
1 potato, peeled and chopped
1½ quarts beef stock

½ cup cream
1 egg yolk
Salt and pepper to taste
Chopped parsley
Sliced tomato

Combine turnip, carrot, potato, and stock in soup kettle. Bring just to a boil, reduce heat, and simmer, partially covered, 30 minutes or until turnip is tender. Press vegetables and liquid through food mill. Return mixture to kettle and heat. In separate bowl combine cream and egg yolk and beat lightly. Add ½ cup hot soup liquid to cream mixture and blend with whisk. Return mixture to kettle. Stir until smooth. Season with salt and pepper. Garnish with chopped parsley and thinly sliced tomato. *Serves 6.*

TURNIP AND CABBAGE SOUP

This simple soup makes a complete meal.

¼ pound salt pork, chopped
3 turnips, peeled and chopped
6 leeks, white parts only,
   sliced

1 head cabbage, cored and
   finely chopped
1½ quarts chicken stock
Salt and pepper to taste

Fry salt pork in soup kettle until crisp. Remove with slotted spoon and set aside. Sauté turnips and leeks in fat until soft. Add cabbage, stir, and sauté until wilted. Add stock and simmer, partially covered, 30 minutes. Season with salt and pepper. If desired, garnish with reserved salt pork. *Serves 8-10.*

CREAM OF VEGETABLE SOUP

Pour (hot or cold) into a thermos and take to work for lunch.

½ bunch broccoli or ½ head
   cauliflower, chopped, or 6
   to 8 Brussels sprouts
2 cups cold water
3 tablespoons butter

2 tablespoons flour
2 cups boiling chicken stock
1 cup cream
Salt and pepper to taste
Chopped walnuts

Combine broccoli, or other vegetable, and water in soup kettle, bring to a boil, reduce heat, cover, and simmer 20 minutes or until tender.

Drain, reserving liquid. Set vegetables aside. Melt butter in heavy saucepan, sprinkle with flour, and blend with whisk over low heat; do not brown. Add hot stock and reserved vegetable cooking liquid and stir until smooth. Add reserved vegetables and simmer, partially covered, 15 minutes. Press mixture through food mill. Return to kettle. Add cream and season with salt and pepper. Reheat but do not boil. Garnish with chopped walnuts. (Also good cold.)

Serves 6-8.

GRANDMOTHER'S VEGETABLE SOUP

Just the thing to simmer on a woodstove in winter.

3 pounds beef bones	1 bay leaf
2½ quarts cold water or beef stock	3 potatoes, peeled and cubed
	3 stalks celery, sliced
1 sprig thyme	2 carrots, peeled and sliced
1 sprig marjoram	1 cup barley
5 peppercorns	Salt and pepper to taste

Combine bones, water, thyme, marjoram, peppercorns, and bay leaf in soup kettle. Simmer, covered, 2½ hours. Remove bones and cut off any remaining bits of meat. Strain stock. Cool, chill, and skim fat from top. Return to kettle with meat. Add vegetables and simmer, partially covered, 15 minutes. Add barley and simmer 10 minutes longer or until barley is tender. Season with salt and pepper.

Serves 6-8.

PUREED VEGETABLE SOUP I

Smooth-textured and simple to make.

1 potato, peeled and sliced	1 cup green or wax beans, cut into 1-inch pieces
1 onion, peeled and sliced	
1 carrot, peeled and sliced	4 sprigs parsley
1 cup chopped spinach or Swiss chard	1½ quarts chicken stock
	Parmesan cheese
2 ripe tomatoes, peeled and sliced	

Soak the vegetables and parsley in cold water to cover for 15 minutes. Take directly from water and place in soup kettle. Do not dry. Simmer, covered, over very low heat 20 minutes. Press through food mill. Return to kettle, add stock, and simmer, partially covered, 30 minutes, stirring occasionally. Garnish with grated Parmesan cheese.

Serves 4-6.

PUREED VEGETABLE SOUP II

For a chunky soup, serve without pureeing.

1 tablespoon butter
1 onion, peeled and chopped
1 stalk celery, sliced
3 potatoes, peeled and sliced
2 carrots, peeled and sliced

2 tablespoons chopped
  parsley
5 cups chicken or beef stock
Salt and pepper to taste
Chopped parsley

Melt butter in soup kettle and sauté onion and celery until tender.
Add remaining vegetables, parsley, and stock; bring to a boil, reduce
heat and simmer, partially covered, 20 minutes or until vegetables
are tender. Puree in food mill, reheat, and season with salt and
pepper. Garnish with chopped parsley.   *Serves 4-6.*

VEGETABLE CHEESE SOUP

*Serve this rich, creamy soup at holiday time, or to make a weekday dinner
special.*

8 tablespoons butter
1 stalk celery, chopped
1 carrot, peeled and chopped
1 onion, peeled and chopped
1 green or sweet red pepper,
  cored and chopped

2 cups chicken stock
3 tablespoons flour
3 cups milk
1 cup cream
1 cup grated cheddar cheese
Salt and pepper to taste

Melt 4 tablespoons butter in heavy skillet or soup kettle. Sauté
celery, carrot, onion, and green pepper until tender. Add stock and
simmer, partially covered, 15 minutes. As vegetables cook melt
remaining 4 tablespoons butter in a saucepan. Stir in flour with
whisk until blended. Over low heat add milk and cream, stirring
constantly until mixture is smooth. Add cheese and season with salt
and pepper. Slowly add cheese mixture to stock and stir until
smooth. Heat gently. Do not boil.   *Serves 6.*

Meat Soups

HARVEST SOUP

This hearty soup will whet the appetite of anyone who smells it cooking.

1 pound ground beef
2 to 3 onions, peeled and
  chopped
4 cups cold water
2 carrots, peeled and sliced
2 stalks celery, chopped
1 to 2 potatoes, peeled and
  chopped

Salt and pepper to taste
1 bay leaf
¼ teaspoon chopped basil
6 fresh tomatoes, peeled and
  chopped, or 1 can (20
  ounces), undrained

Brown meat in skillet. Drain, leaving 1 tablespoon fat. Set meat aside. Sauté onions in fat until tender. Combine onions with all ingredients except tomatoes in soup kettle, heat to a boil, reduce heat, cover, and simmer 30 minutes. Return meat to soup, add tomatoes, and simmer another 10 minutes or until vegetables are tender.

Serves 6.

POOR MAN'S SOUP

Hardly an appropriate title in view of today's prices for ground beef, but this soup was a budget meal in New England several decades ago.

1 pound lean ground beef
2 teaspoons chopped oregano
2 quarts beef stock
4 carrots, peeled and chopped

2 turnips, peeled and chopped
3 stalks celery, chopped
2 onions, peeled and chopped
¼ cup barley

Combine beef and oregano and roll into walnut-sized balls. Set aside. Combine remaining ingredients in soup kettle and simmer 5 minutes. Add meatballs and simmer, partially covered, 30 minutes longer, or until all vegetables are tender.

Serves 6-8.

VEGETABLE-BEEF SOUP

No canned soup by the same name can compare.

1 pound beef shank
2 quarts beef stock or water
2 onions, peeled and chopped
1 sprig thyme
2 carrots, peeled and chopped
2 stalks celery, chopped

2 potatoes, peeled and
  chopped
1 cup fresh green beans, cut
  into 1-inch pieces
1 tablespoon chopped parsley
2 cups tomato or V-8 juice

Combine beef, stock, onions, and thyme in soup kettle. Simmer over low heat, partially covered, 2 hours. Skim occasionally. Remove beef, cool, cut meat from bones, and set aside. Cool broth, then chill and skim. Return broth and meat to kettle. Heat to simmer. Add remaining ingredients, simmer, partially covered, 20 minutes or until vegetables are tender, and serve hot. *Serves 6-8.*

SPICY VEGETABLE SOUP

Accompanied by homemade bread, this full-bodied, sharp-flavored soup makes a complete meal.

3 onions, peeled and sliced
6 stalks celery and leaves,
  chopped
5 fresh tomatoes, peeled and
  chopped
1 pound stew beef, cut into 1-
  inch cubes
2 tablespoons tomato paste
2 cloves garlic, minced
10 peppercorns
2 teaspoons caraway seed
2 bay leaves

5 whole cloves
Cold water
2 tomatoes, peeled and
  chopped
1 parsnip or ¼ turnip, peeled
  and chopped
1 carrot, peeled and chopped
1 potato, peeled and chopped
2 tablespoons lemon juice
Salt and pepper to taste
Yogurt or sour cream

Combine first 10 ingredients in soup kettle. Add cold water to cover and simmer, covered, 2 hours. Strain soup through sieve. Return beef to broth but discard cooked vegetables and spices. Add remaining fresh vegetables along with lemon juice and cook 20 minutes or until tender. Season with salt and pepper. Garnish with yogurt or sour cream. *Serves 6-8.*

OXTAIL SOUP

Oxtail makes a flavorful soup meat that readily separates from the bones when tender.

2 quarts beef stock	2 stalks celery, chopped
1 pound oxtail sections	1 onion, peeled and chopped
½ cup barley	1 cup sliced mushrooms
2 tablespoons butter	Salt and pepper to taste
3 carrots, peeled and chopped	Chopped parsley

Combine stock and oxtail in soup kettle and simmer, partially covered, 2 hours. Skim occasionally during cooking. Remove from heat. Cut meat from bones and chop. Set aside meat and discard bones. Cool stock, chill, and skim fat from top. Return meat and stock to kettle. Heat to simmer. Add barley and cook 15 minutes. As barley cooks, melt butter in small skillet and sauté carrots, celery, onion, and mushrooms 5 minutes. Add to soup and season with salt and pepper. Simmer 10 minutes longer. Garnish with chopped parsley. *Serves 4.*

OXTAIL AND PEPPER SOUP

Hits the spot on those bone-chilling days.

2 pounds oxtail sections	3 onions, peeled and sliced
2½ quarts cold water or beef stock	2 cloves garlic, minced
3 tablespoons butter	2 tablespoons flour
4 green peppers, cored and chopped	Sour cream

Combine oxtail and water in soup kettle. Bring to a boil, reduce heat, and simmer, covered, 2 hours. Remove tail, chop meat, and discard bones. Cool stock, chill, and skim fat from top. Combine meat and stock in clean kettle and simmer 5 minutes. Melt butter in skillet and sauté green peppers, onions, and garlic until soft. Sprinkle with flour and stir until blended. Add several cups hot stock from kettle and stir until smooth. Add sautéed vegetables mixture to kettle and simmer 20 minutes. Garnish with sour cream. *Serves 6-8.*

LAMB AND BARLEY SOUP

Delicious with hot biscuits.

2 pounds meaty lamb bones
2 quarts cold water
5 peppercorns
2 carrots, peeled and chopped
½ turnip, peeled and chopped
2 to 3 onions, peeled and
   chopped
2 cloves garlic, minced
¼ cup chopped parsley
¼ cup barley
Salt and pepper to taste
Parsley

Combine bones, water, and peppercorns in soup kettle. Bring to a boil, reduce heat, and simmer, covered, 2 hours. Strain. Pick meat off bones and add meat to kettle. Add vegetables and herbs and simmer, partially covered, 30 minutes. Add barley and simmer, partially covered, 15 minutes or until tender. Season with salt and pepper. Garnish with parsley.   *Serves 6-8.*

Poultry, Fish, and Seafood Soups

CHICKEN ALMOND SOUP

This chicken soup has a special texture and taste.

4 cups chicken stock
¼ cup cooked, finely chopped
　white chicken meat
2 whole cloves
1 stalk celery, chopped
1 carrot, peeled and chopped

1 bay leaf
2 leaves fresh basil
1 cup blanched almonds
Salt and pepper to taste
Toasted almonds, grated
　lemon peel, or watercress

Combine stock, chicken, cloves, celery, carrot, bay leaf, and basil in soup kettle. Bring to a boil, reduce heat, and simmer, partially covered, 30 minutes. Remove bay leaf and cloves. Press mixture through food mill. Return to soup kettle. Grind almonds in blender and add to kettle. Stir well and simmer 10 minutes. Season with salt and pepper. Serve hot, garnished with toasted, sliced almonds; or serve cold, with grated lemon peel or watercress. *Serves 6-8.*

CHICKEN AND LEEK SOUP

Cock-a-Leekie, as the Scottish call it, needs the subtle flavor of leeks to make it just right. But in a pinch, onions will work reasonably well.

1 small stewing chicken with
　giblets
2 quarts cold water
Bouquet garni (see pages 15-16)

6 whole leeks, sliced
Salt and pepper to taste
Parsley

Combine chicken and giblets with water in soup kettle. Add *bouquet garni*. Bring to a boil, skim, reduce heat, and simmer, covered, 2 hours. Discard herbs and remove chicken. Cool, skin, and cut meat into bite-sized pieces. Discard skin and bones. Cool stock, chill, and skim fat from top. Return stock and chicken to kettle. Simmer 5 minutes. Add leeks and simmer, partially covered, 20 minutes longer. Season with salt and pepper. Garnish with parsley.
Serves 6-8.

CHICKEN AND LEMON SOUP

Use a rich chicken stock as the base for this soup.

1½ quarts chicken stock
2 onions, peeled and chopped
¼ cup freshly squeezed lemon
  juice

2 cups chopped, cooked
  chicken
Chopped dill

Combine stock and onions in soup kettle and simmer 20 minutes, partially covered. Add lemon juice and chicken, stir, and heat thoroughly. Garnish with chopped dill. *Serves 4-6.*

CHICKEN AND LENTIL SOUP

Serve as a main dish, followed by a salad.

1 pound chicken parts (wings,
  thighs, etc.)
2½ quarts cold water
1 cup lentils
1 bay leaf

2 tablespoons butter
2 onions, peeled and chopped
1 cup uncooked rice
Salt and pepper to taste

Combine chicken and water in soup kettle. Bring just to a boil, reduce heat, cover, and simmer 45 minutes. Remove chicken, cool, discard skin, pull meat from bones, and chop. Set aside. Chill stock and skim fat from top. Return stock and chicken to kettle and heat to simmer. Add lentils and bay leaf and simmer, partially covered, 20 minutes. As lentils cook, melt butter in small skillet and sauté onions until tender. Add to chicken and lentils along with rice. Cover and cook slowly 20 minutes or until rice is tender. Remove bay leaf and season with salt and pepper. *Serves 6-8.*

CHICKEN NOODLE SOUP

Nothing artificial here — from stock to noodles to final product.

1½ quarts chicken stock
1 pound chicken wings and
  thighs
2 carrots, peeled and chopped

1 tablespoon chopped parsley
1 cup uncooked noodles
Salt and pepper to taste

Combine stock and chicken in soup kettle. Simmer 1 hour, partially covered. Remove chicken, cool, discard skin and bones, chop meat. Cool broth, chill, and skim fat from top. Reheat broth in kettle, add chicken, carrots, and parsley. Simmer 10 minutes. Add noodles and simmer until tender. Season with salt and pepper. *Serves 4.*

CHICKEN AND RICE SOUP

This soup is easy to make and a good way to use up leftover chicken.

1½ quarts chicken stock
2 stalks celery, sliced
2 tablespoons chopped
  parsley

1 carrot, peeled and chopped
1 cup cooked rice
1 to 2 cups chopped, cooked
  chicken

Combine stock, celery, parsley, carrot, and rice in soup kettle and simmer, partially covered, 10 minutes. Add chicken and heat thoroughly.   *Serves 6-8.*

CREAM OF CHICKEN SOUP

With a rich stock, you can omit the meat and still enjoy good chicken flavor.

3 tablespoons butter
2 tablespoons flour
4 cups chicken stock
2 cups cream
2 egg yolks, beaten

Salt and pepper to taste
2 cups diced, white chicken
  meat
Chopped parsley

Melt butter in soup kettle. Add flour and cook over low heat, stirring constantly until blended. Slowly add stock and stir until smooth. Heat almost to a boil. In separate bowl combine cream and egg yolks. Pour ½ cup of hot soup into cream and egg mixture. Blend with whisk and return mixture to kettle. Season with salt and pepper. Add chicken meat and heat but do not boil. Garnish with chopped parsley.   *Serves 6.*

MICHAEL'S CHICKEN SOUP

Feed to someone sick and watch the speedy recovery.

2 quarts chicken stock
½ cup dry vermouth
2 carrots, peeled and chopped
2 stalks celery, chopped
1 bay leaf
½ cup uncooked macaroni

¼ teaspoon tarragon, or
  ½ teaspoon dill
Juice of ½ lemon
Salt and pepper to taste
Parsley

Combine stock, vermouth, carrots, celery, and bay leaf in soup kettle. Cover and simmer 20 minutes. Increase heat, add macaroni, and cook 10 minutes. Add tarragon or dill, lemon juice, and salt and pepper. Garnish with parsley, and serve with rye bread.   *Serves 6-8.*

TURKEY SOUP

A recipe that makes the most of your leftover holiday turkey.

2 tablespoons butter
2 onions, peeled and chopped
2 green peppers, cored and
    chopped
4 cups turkey stock
2 cups canned Italian plum
    tomatoes, drained and
    chopped

2 cups chopped turkey
2 tablespoons chopped
    parsley
Salt and pepper to taste
2 cups cooked rice

Melt butter in heavy skillet and sauté onions and green peppers until soft. Add stock, tomatoes, turkey, and parsley. Simmer, partially covered, 15 minutes. Season with salt and pepper. Add rice, stir, and heat thoroughly. *Serves 4-6.*

CLAM AND SPINACH SOUP

Serve as a main dish for lunch or supper.

¼ pound salt pork, diced
2 onions, chopped
1 clove garlic, minced
1 pound spinach, chopped
5 tablespoons butter

2 tablespoons flour
4 cups clam stock
2 cups minced clams
1 cup cream

Fry salt pork in soup kettle until crisp. Remove with slotted spoon and set aside. Sauté onions and garlic in fat until tender. Add spinach, cover, and simmer until wilted. Melt butter in separate saucepan. Add flour and stir over low heat until blended. Slowly add stock, stirring, and heat. Pour mixture into kettle and stir until smooth. Add clams and cream and heat. Do not boil. *Serves 6-8.*

CRAB SOUP

Crabs that inhabit New England waters have hard shells and you must spend hours cleaning them to get enough meat for a meal. But the labor is worth the effort. Steam crabs as you would lobsters and pick out the meat when the shells turn bright red.

3 cups cooked crab meat
3 cups clam stock
1 tablespoon Worcestershire
    sauce
1 teaspoon lemon juice

3 tablespoons butter
4 cups cream
¼ cup sherry
Salt and pepper to taste
Paprika

Combine crab meat, stock, Worcestershire sauce, lemon juice, and butter in soup kettle. Simmer several minutes until butter melts, stirring slowly. Add cream and sherry and heat thoroughly. Season with salt and pepper. Garnish with a sprinkling of paprika. *Serves 6-8.*

CRAB AND TOMATO BISQUE

For a smooth bisque, press tomatoes through a food mill before adding to the soup.

2 tablespoons butter
2 tablespoons flour
2 cups milk or cream
½ teaspoon salt
⅛ teaspoon pepper
1 cup (6-ounce can) flaked
    crab meat

1 cup peeled, canned
    tomatoes, mashed, with
    juice
Chopped parsley

Melt butter in saucepan. Over low heat add flour slowly, and blend with whisk. Add milk gradually and cook until mixture thickens, stirring constantly. Add seasonings and crab meat and simmer several minutes. Just before serving heat tomatoes and juice in separate pan. When tomatoes are hot, gradually add to soup and serve immediately. Garnish with chopped parsley.   *Serves 4.*

FISH SOUP

Use fresh herbs if possible.

3½ quarts cold water
2 pounds fish frames (heads, tails, bones)
2 stalks celery, sliced
2 large onions, peeled and sliced
2 sprigs thyme
1 bay leaf

2 cups dry white wine
2 tablespoons butter
3 carrots, peeled and sliced
1 clove garlic, minced
¼ cup chopped chives
½ cup tomato puree
French bread
Chives

Combine water, fish frames, celery, onions, thyme, bay leaf, and 1 cup wine in soup kettle. Bring to a boil, reduce heat, and simmer, uncovered, 30 minutes. As stock is cooking, melt butter in second kettle, and add carrots, garlic, and chives. Pour in remaining wine, cover, and simmer 10 minutes. Strain fish stock into cooked carrots and chives. Pick any remaining bits of meat from bones and add to soup. Stir in tomato puree and heat thoroughly. Ladle into bowls and top with toasted French bread and a sprinkling of chives.

Serves 4-6.

HALIBUT AND TOMATO SOUP

Time carefully so you don't overcook the fish.

3 strips of bacon, diced
1 onion, peeled and chopped
2 cups fish stock
¼ cup uncooked rice

1 pound halibut, skinned, boned, and cubed
2 cups tomato juice
2 teaspoons chopped dill

Fry bacon in soup kettle until crisp. Remove with slotted spoon and set aside. Sauté onion in fat until tender. Add stock and rice. Cover and simmer 10 minutes. Add fish and simmer, partially covered, 10 minutes longer or until tender. Add tomato juice and dill and heat thoroughly. Garnish with reserved bacon.

Serves 4.

FISH AND SPINACH SOUP

Grated carrot supplies an interesting bit of color.

3 cups chopped spinach	*Bouquet garni* (see pages 15-16)
5 cups chicken stock or water	2 peppercorns
4 tablespoons butter	Salt and pepper
2 onions, peeled and grated	¼ cup dry white wine
1 carrot, peeled and grated	1 pound flounder fillets, cut
1 tablespoon flour	into 2- to 3-inch pieces

Combine spinach and ½ cup stock in saucepan. Bring to a boil, reduce heat, and simmer, uncovered, 5 minutes. Press through food mill and set aside. Melt 2 tablespoons butter in soup kettle, sauté onions and carrot until tender. Sprinkle with flour and blend with whisk. Slowly add remaining 4½ cups stock and stir until smooth. Add pureed spinach, *bouquet garni*, and peppercorns. Season with salt and pepper to taste. Bring just to a boil, reduce heat, and simmer, partially covered, 10 minutes. Heat remaining 2 table-spoons butter in skillet. Add wine, bring mixture to a boil, reduce heat. Add flounder, cover, and simmer 5 minutes. Spoon flounder into soup bowls and cover with hot soup.   *Serves 4.*

MOCK LOBSTER BISQUE

Here's a way to get every penny's worth out of lobsters.

2 lobster shells (claws, tails, backs)	1 tablespoon butter
4 cups fish stock or water	1 small onion, peeled and chopped
Salt and pepper to taste	1 tablespoon flour
2 sprigs parsley	½ cup cream

Crush lobster shells into small pieces. Place in soup kettle along with stock, salt and pepper, and parsley. Bring just to a boil, reduce heat, and simmer, partially covered, 2 hours. Strain through cheesecloth. Reserve broth, discard shells. Melt butter in second kettle. Sauté onion until soft. Sprinkle with flour and blend with whisk. Slowly add lobster broth, stirring constantly. Remove from heat, add cream, and reheat. Do not boil.   *Serves 4-6.*

FRESH PEA SOUP WITH SHRIMP

Shrimp adds a special touch to this soup. Use frozen shrimp if you can't obtain fresh.

4½ cups chicken stock
¼ pound salt pork
2 carrots, peeled and sliced
2 onions, sliced
1 teaspoon chopped summer
    savory

2 cups fresh peas, or 1 package
    (10 ounces) frozen
½ cup cooked shrimp
½ cup white wine

Combine stock, salt pork, carrots, and onions in soup kettle. Boil 10 minutes. Discard salt pork. Add summer savory and peas. Simmer, partially covered, 10 minutes or until peas are tender. Press mixture through food mill and return to kettle. Add shrimp and wine and heat thoroughly. *Serves 4.*

PUMPKIN-OYSTER SOUP

An attractive soup for holidays and special occasions; serve with oyster crackers on the side.

2 tablespoons butter
3 stalks celery, chopped
2 onions, peeled and chopped
1 cup mashed, cooked
    pumpkin
4 cups chicken stock

1 cup cream
1 cup oysters, drained of
    liquor
Salt and pepper to taste
Parsley

Melt butter in soup kettle. Sauté celery and onions until tender. Remove from heat, stir in pumpkin and stock. Heat slowly, add cream, and stir until blended. Add oysters, season with salt and pepper, and cook gently about 10 minutes, or until oysters are heated through. Do not boil. Garnish with parsley. *Serves 6.*

SALMON SOUP

A tasty way to use up leftover salmon.

1 salmon frame (head, tail, bones)
4 to 6 quarts cold water
3 onions, peeled and sliced
2 carrots, peeled and sliced
4 peppercorns
1 bay leaf
4 potatoes, peeled and chopped
1 leek, white part only, chopped
Fresh dill

Combine salmon frame, water, onions, carrots, peppercorns, and bay leaf in soup kettle. (If necessary, cut frame into several pieces so it will fit.) Bring to a boil, reduce heat, and simmer, partially covered, 20 minutes. Strain stock through cheesecloth and pour into clean soup kettle. Discard any remaining fish skin and pick bits of meat from bones. Add to stock. Add potatoes, cover, and simmer 15 minutes. Add leek and cook 5 minutes longer. Garnish with fresh dill.   *Serves 6-8.*

SEAFOOD BISQUE

A rich, thick soup.

½ pound haddock, skinned, boned, and cut into 1-inch pieces
½ pound fresh shrimp
1 bay leaf
4 tablespoons butter
½ pound scallops (if large scallops are used, cut into pieces)
½ cup flaked crab meat
2 cups cream
1 cup milk
Paprika

Place haddock in saucepan, add water to cover, and simmer 10 minutes. In separate pan boil shrimp in water to cover with bay leaf 10 minutes. Drain and remove shells. Melt butter in soup kettle, sauté scallops 10 minutes over low heat. Add shrimp, drained haddock, and crab meat and cook, stirring occasionally, over low heat 15 minutes. Add cream and milk and heat thoroughly, but do not boil. Garnish with paprika.   *Serves 4-6.*

IV.
Cold Soups

Fruit Soups

BLACKBERRY SOUP

Serve in small bowls as an appetizer on a hot summer night, or as a dessert soup, generously garnished with whipped cream. You can also use black raspberries, if available.

4 cups blackberries, fresh or
  frozen, thawed and drained
2 cups cold water
½ lemon, sliced

¼ cup sugar
3 whole cloves
2-inch stick cinnamon
½ cup cream

Set aside a few berries to use as a garnish. Combine berries, water, lemon, sugar, cloves, and cinnamon in soup kettle. Simmer, mashing berries with a spoon, until fruit is soft. Strain through a fine sieve, pressing to remove as much juice as possible. Cool, chill well, and blend in cream. Garnish with berries or whipped cream, or both.   *Serves 6-8.*

BLUEBERRY SOUP

Try wild blueberries, or if cultivated berries are your only choice, use fruit juice instead of water for additional flavor.

2 cups blueberries, fresh or
  dry-frozen
3 cups water, grape juice, or
  cranberry juice
¼ to ½ cup sugar
½ lemon, sliced

2-inch to 4-inch stick
  cinnamon
½ cup dry white wine
  (optional)
1 cup cream or sour cream
Sour cream or whipped cream

Combine berries, water or juice, sugar, lemon, cinnamon, and wine in saucepan. Bring just to a boil, reduce heat, and simmer 25 minutes, partially covered. Remove lemon slices and cinnamon stick and press mixture through food mill. Cool and chill. Add cream and stir until smooth. Garnish with additional sour cream or whipped cream.   *Serves 6.*

HUNGARIAN CHERRY SOUP

For a smooth soup, puree in a blender. Serve as an appetizer or as a dessert.

3 cups cold water
1 cup sugar
2-inch to 4-inch stick
 cinnamon
4 cups pitted sour cherries (if
 canned, drain)
1 tablespoon arrowroot

2 tablespoons cold water
¼ cup cream
¾ cup dry red wine, chilled
Lemon peel or sour cream; or
 whipped cream and
 powdered cinnamon

Combine water, sugar, and cinnamon in soup kettle. Bring to a boil and add cherries. Simmer, partially covered, over low heat 35 to 40 minutes if cherries are fresh, 10 minutes if canned. Remove cinnamon stick. Mix arrowroot and 2 tablespoons cold water to form a paste. Beat into soup until smooth. Increase heat and stir constantly until soup boils. Reduce heat and simmer 2 minutes or until slightly thick. Cool and chill. Before serving add cream and wine and stir. If served as an appetizer, garnish with lemon peel or sour cream; as a dessert, top with whipped cream and sprinkle with cinnamon. *Serves 6.*

CRANBERRY SOUP

The color of strawberry ice cream, this is a versatile soup. If desired, omit club soda and garnish with sour cream and pecans.

2 oranges
1 tablespoon butter
1½ cups sugar
1 cup sherry
1 pound fresh or frozen
 cranberries (if cranberries
 are not available, omit
 sugar and use a 16-ounce

can whole or jellied
 cranberry sauce)
1 cup dry white wine (dry
 sauterne)
1 cup cream
1 cup sour cream
1 cup club soda
Pecan halves

Peel rind off oranges and cut rind into fine strips. Juice oranges and set juice aside. Melt butter in saucepan. Sauté orange rind for several minutes; do not brown. Add sugar, sherry, and orange juice. Boil uncovered 2 minutes. Add cranberries, cover, and boil 2 more minutes. Uncover and boil 3 minutes longer. Cool and chill. Puree in blender with white wine. Add cream and sour cream and blend 1 minute more. Strain out orange rind and cranberry seeds. Before serving add club soda and mix well. Chill. Garnish with pecan halves. *Serves 6-8.*

EGG AND LEMON SOUP

In Greek communities, this soup is known as Avgolemono.

1½ quarts clarified chicken
   stock
½ cup uncooked rice

3 egg yolks
Juice of 1 lemon
Lemon slices

Combine stock and rice in soup kettle, cover tightly, and simmer 20 minutes. (Don't peek at rice as it cooks.) Remove from heat. In small bowl combine egg yolks and lemon juice. Beat with whisk until smooth. Pour 1 cup hot soup into egg and lemon mixture, stirring slowly and constantly until blended. Return mixture to soup kettle and continue stirring slowly for several minutes over low heat until mixture is smooth. (Do not let soup boil after egg and lemon have been added or it will curdle.) Cool, chill, and serve cold, garnished with paper-thin slices of lemon. (Also good hot.) *Serves 6-8.*

ELDERBERRY SOUP

Elderberries grow along many New England roadsides and are a long-time favorite for jelly and pie. Increase the sugar if this recipe is too tart for your taste.

4 cups elderberries
1½ quarts water
Juice of ½ lemon
2 tablespoons cornstarch

3 tablespoons water
½ cup sugar
Sour cream

Combine berries and water in soup kettle. Simmer, partially covered, until berries are soft, about 10 minutes. Press mixture through food mill. Return juice to kettle. Combine lemon juice, cornstarch, and water to form a smooth paste. Stir into soup until smooth. Add sugar and stir. Cool, chill, and serve cold, garnished with sour cream. *Serves 6-8.*

FRUIT SOUP

Tastes best served several hours or a day after it is made. Use freshly extracted Concord grape juice or bottled juice, and fresh fruits or canned.

2 cups grape juice
¼ cup lemon juice
2 lemon slices
½ cup sugar
3 whole cloves
2-inch stick cinnamon
Pea-sized piece of whole ginger
3 pear halves, peeled and sliced
2 peach halves, peeled and sliced
6 apricot halves, peeled and sliced
6 plum halves, peeled and sliced, or 6 prunes, halved and stoned
½ cup black or red cherries, halved and stoned

Combine grape and lemon juices, lemon slices, sugar, cloves, cinnamon, and ginger in soup kettle. Simmer 10 minutes, partially covered. As juices cook combine remaining ingredients in saucepan, cover with cold water, and simmer, partially covered, until soft. Cool. Stir cooked fruits and 1 cup cooking liquid into juices in soup kettle. (If canned fruits are used, add along with 1 cup of syrup.) Cool and chill. *Serves 6.*

RASPBERRY-SHERRY SOUP

Refreshing as a first course or as a dessert.

1½ cups water
3 tablespoons quick-cooking tapioca
2 cups grape juice
2 cups pineapple juice
½ cup sugar
Rind of 1 lemon, grated
2-inch stick cinnamon
1 cup fresh raspberries
½ cup sherry

Bring water to a boil in soup kettle. Stir in tapioca and cook until mixture is clear, stirring frequently. Add grape and pineapple juices, bring to a boil, and add sugar, lemon rind, and cinnamon. Reduce heat and simmer 10 minutes. Remove from heat and add raspberries and sherry. Cool, chill, and serve cold. *Serves 4-6.*

STRAWBERRY SOUP

Serve in small cups to begin a summer meal, or present as a light dessert following a large meal.

2 cups fresh strawberries,
   hulled and sliced
Juice of 1 lemon
4 whole cloves
1 sprig marjoram
1 cup water

¼ cup sugar
1 cup dry red wine
½ cup sour cream or yogurt
Sliced strawberries, mint
   leaves, and sour cream

Combine strawberries, lemon juice, cloves, marjoram, and water in saucepan. Simmer 10 minutes. Press through food mill and return to saucepan. Add sugar and wine, stir, bring just to a boil, reduce heat, and simmer 5 minutes. Cool and chill. Fold in sour cream or yogurt and serve. Garnish with strawberry slices, fresh mint leaves, and, if desired, extra sour cream. *Serves 4.*

STRAWBERRY-RHUBARB SOUP

This special blend of flavors works as well in soup as it does in pie.

6 cups rhubarb, cut into
   1-inch pieces
2 cups strawberries, hulled
   and sliced
1½ quarts water
2 tablespoons cornstarch

¼ cup cold water or dry white
   wine
¼ cup sugar (or more to taste)
1 cup cream
1 egg yolk
Sliced strawberries

Combine rhubarb, strawberries, and water in soup kettle and simmer, partially covered, 20 minutes. Strain, reserving fruits, and return liquid to kettle. Reheat to simmer. Combine cornstarch and water or wine to form a smooth paste. Add ½ cup hot soup to paste, stir with a whisk until blended, and add mixture to kettle. Cook over low heat, stirring constantly, until smooth. Add sugar and reserved fruits and stir. Combine cream and egg yolk and stir slowly into soup. Do not boil. Cool, chill, and serve cold, garnished with additional sliced berries. (Also good hot.) *Serves 6-8.*

Vegetable Soups

AVOCADO SOUP

Make a meal of this luscious creamy soup, a spinach salad, and French bread.

3 very ripe avocados, peeled,
  seeded, and chopped
1½ quarts chicken stock
4 shallots or 1 small onion,
  peeled and coarsely
  chopped

Salt and pepper to taste
Dash of Tabasco
1½ cups yogurt
½ cup cream
Fresh tomato
Parsley sprigs

Combine avocados, stock, shallots, salt and pepper, and Tabasco in large bowl. Puree in blender, 2 cups at a time, until smooth. Return to bowl and blend in yogurt and cream with whisk. Chill. Garnish with chopped fresh tomato and parsley. *Serves 6-8.*

COLD BEAN SOUP

A refreshing way to enjoy bean soup.

1 cup dry white beans
2 tablespoons butter
1 stalk celery, chopped
2 onions, peeled and chopped
5 cups chicken stock (less if
  beans aren't drained)
3 cloves garlic, minced
Salt and pepper

2 egg yolks
½ cup sour cream
4 tablespoons chopped
  summer savory and/or
  parsley
Sliced tomato or chopped
  parsley

Soak beans overnight in cold water to cover. (Drain or not, as you prefer.) Melt butter in soup kettle, and sauté celery and onions until soft, but not brown. Add stock, beans, and garlic. Cook, uncovered, 1½ hours or until beans are tender. Press through food mill. Add salt and pepper to taste. Beat egg yolks and stir in sour cream. Add ½ cup hot soup to egg and cream mixture and stir until blended. Return mixture to kettle, stirring constantly. If soup is thicker than desired, thin with milk. Remove from heat and add herbs. Chill. Garnish with tomato or additional parsley. *Serves 4-6.*

YOGURT BORSCHT

Use fresh beets, if possible, in this rosy pink soup.

4 to 5 baby beets	2 tablespoons chives
2 carrots, peeled and chopped	1 cup yogurt
1 cucumber, peeled and	1 clove garlic
chopped	Beets, carrots, and parsley for
3 cups chicken stock	garnish

Combine ingredients in blender and puree. Chill thoroughly.
Garnish with chilled, minced beets and carrots, and a sprinkling of
parsley.   *Serves 4.*

CUCUMBER SOUP

Lovely for lunch on a sultry summer day.

½ cup walnuts	2 cucumbers, peeled, seeded,
2 cloves garlic	and chopped
3 tablespoons dry white wine	Salt and pepper
2 cups yogurt	Chopped walnuts or dill
½ cup milk	

Puree walnuts, garlic, and wine in blender. Combine yogurt and
milk in bowl and stir in pureed nut mixture. Add cucumbers. Thin
with additional milk to desired consistency, then season with salt
and pepper to taste. Chill thoroughly. Garnish with chopped nuts or
dill.   *Serves 4.*

CREAM OF CUCUMBER SOUP

An unusual soup that resembles vichyssoise.

2 tablespoons butter	1 quart milk
2 or 3 cucumbers, peeled and	2 onion slices
chopped	½ teaspoon mace
4 stalks celery with leaves,	1 cup cream
chopped	2 egg yolks, slightly beaten
3 tablespoons flour	Salt and pepper
3 cups hot chicken stock	Chopped chives

Melt butter in soup kettle. Sauté cucumbers and celery until tender.
Sprinkle with flour and stir until blended. Gradually add stock,
stirring constantly, until mixture is smooth. Scald milk, onion, and
mace in separate pan. Add milk mixture to kettle, and heat just to a
boil. Combine cream and egg yolks in a bowl. Stir ½ cup of hot soup
into egg and cream mixture and return mixture to kettle. Season to
taste with salt and pepper. Cool and chill. Serve cold, garnished with
chopped chives.   *Serves 6-8.*

CUCUMBER-SPINACH SOUP

Don't overcook the spinach or it will lose its bright green color.

4 cups beef stock
1 onion, peeled and chopped
2 cucumbers, peeled, seeded,
  and chopped
2 carrots, peeled and chopped
1 bay leaf
1 tablespoon chopped
  summer savory

1 potato, peeled and chopped
2 cups chopped spinach
Salt and pepper to taste
2 cups sour cream
Chopped cucumber

Combine stock, onion, cucumbers, carrots, bay leaf, and summer savory in soup kettle. Simmer, partially covered, 15 minutes over low heat. In separate saucepan boil potato 15 minutes or until tender. In another pan boil or steam spinach for several minutes. Remove bay leaf from vegetables in kettle. Combine drained potato and drained spinach with other vegetables and press through food mill. Season with salt and pepper. Cool, chill, and stir in sour cream. Serve cold, garnished with chopped cucumber.   *Serves 6.*

EGGPLANT SOUP

A tasty blend of eggplant and yogurt, accented by a touch of mint.

4 tablespoons oil
3 small eggplants, peeled and
  cubed
1 sweet red pepper, cored and
  chopped
1 clove garlic, minced

½ cup chicken stock
2 cups yogurt
1 cup milk or cream
Salt and pepper
Mint leaves

Heat oil in skillet and sauté eggplant, pepper, and garlic 5 minutes. Add stock, cover, and simmer 30 minutes over low heat, or until eggplant is soft. Press through food mill. Cool. Add yogurt and milk or cream. Season with salt and pepper to taste. Chill. Garnish with fresh mint leaves.   *Serves 4-6.*

GAZPACHO I

On a very hot day, serve with an ice cube in each bowl.

1 small onion, peeled and
    chopped
2 stalks celery, chopped
1 cucumber, peeled and
    chopped
1 green pepper, cored and
    chopped
4 ripe tomatoes, peeled and
    chopped

1 sprig parsley
1 cup tomato or V-8 juice
1 cup dry white wine
½ teaspoon cumin powder
2 tablespoons olive oil
1 tablespoon lemon juice
2 cloves garlic
Chopped cucumber or chives

Combine all ingredients except garnish in a large bowl. Puree a few cupfuls at a time in blender. Thin with additional tomato juice, if desired. Chill overnight. Garnish with bits of chopped cucumber or chives. *Serves 6.*

GAZPACHO II

In this crunchier version, vegetables are chopped by hand. Dice them as carefully as you can for the best appearance.

1 to 2 cloves garlic, minced
4 ripe tomatoes, peeled and
    finely chopped
1 cucumber, peeled and finely
    chopped
1 sweet onion, peeled and
    finely chopped

1 cup tomato juice
1 green pepper, cored and
    finely chopped
⅓ cup green olives, chopped
    (optional)
1 tablespoon wine vinegar
1 tablespoon oil

Combine all ingredients in a bowl. Refrigerate at least 6 hours before serving. *Serves 4.*

GARLIC SOUP

When you serve this soup, see if your dinner guests can identify the flavor.

4 cups chicken stock
3 cloves garlic, crushed
2 cups cream
2 egg yolks

Dash of Tabasco
Salt and pepper to taste
Chopped chives

Combine stock and garlic in soup kettle and simmer, partially covered, 30 minutes. Strain out garlic and return broth to kettle. In a bowl blend cream and egg yolks. Add ½ cup hot stock to egg and cream mixture, blend with whisk, and return mixture to kettle. Simmer 5 minutes. Season with Tabasco and salt and pepper. Cool, chill, and serve cold. Garnish with chopped chives.   *Serves 6.*

POTATO AND TOMATO SOUP

An end-of-the-garden soup for an Indian summer day.

4 tomatoes, peeled, seeded,
    and chopped
¼ cup tomato juice
¼ cup chopped basil
3 carrots, peeled and chopped
3 potatoes, peeled and
    chopped

3 cups chicken stock
1 onion, peeled and chopped
1 clove garlic, minced
1 cup cream
Salt and pepper to taste
Tomato slices

Combine tomatoes, tomato juice, basil, and carrots in saucepan and simmer, covered, over low heat until carrots are tender. Press through food mill and chill. Combine potatoes, stock, onion, and garlic in separate saucepan and simmer, partially covered, 20 minutes or until potatoes are tender. Puree in food mill. Add cream and cold tomato mixture and chill. Season with salt and pepper. Garnish with thin slices of fresh tomato.   *Serves 4-6.*

SQUASH SOUP

A light, warm-weather soup.

6 small yellow squash, chopped	¼ cup chopped parsley
2 quarts chicken stock	½ teaspoon salt
2 cloves garlic, minced	½ cup sour cream
½ teaspoon oregano	Dill

Combine squash, stock, garlic, oregano, parsley, and salt in soup kettle. Cover and simmer 15 minutes. Press mixture through food mill. Cool. Stir in sour cream until smooth. Chill. Garnish with fresh dill.   *Serves 6-8.*

VICHY SQUASH SOUP

Use small squash four to eight inches long for the best flavor.

4 tablespoons butter	1 cup cream (or ½ cup cream,
1 onion, peeled and sliced	½ cup milk)
6 summer squash, chopped	Salt and pepper
½ cup beef or chicken stock	

Melt butter in heavy skillet and sauté onion until tender. Add squash and stock, cover, and simmer 10 minutes or until vegetables are tender. Press through food mill. Add cream and salt and pepper to taste. Cool, chill, and serve cold.   *Serves 4.*

VICHYSSOISE I

This classic cold soup of all time was first served at the Ritz Hotel in New York City.

2 tablespoons butter	4 cups cold water
6 leeks, white parts only, chopped	2 cups milk
1 onion, peeled and chopped	1 cup cream
4 to 5 potatoes, peeled and chopped	Chopped chives

Melt butter in soup kettle. Sauté leeks and onion until tender. Do not brown. Add potatoes and water and simmer until potatoes are cooked. Press through food mill. Stir in milk and cool. Add cream and chill. Garnish with chopped chives.   *Serves 6.*

VICHYSSOISE II

This version calls for celery and a splash of white wine.

4 tablespoons butter
4 leeks, white parts only,
    sliced
2 onions, peeled and sliced
2 stalks celery, sliced
1½ quarts chicken stock

2 potatoes, peeled and
    chopped
1 cup cream
¼ cup dry white wine
Salt and pepper to taste
Chopped chives

Melt butter in soup kettle. Sauté leeks, onions, and celery until tender. Add stock and potatoes, simmer 15 minutes or until potatoes are tender. Press through food mill. Return to kettle, add cream and wine. Stir over low heat until smooth. Season with salt and pepper. Cool, chill, and serve cold, garnished with chopped chives.

Serves 6-8.

ZUCCHINI SOUP

Summer squash may be substituted in this recipe.

4 potatoes, peeled and
    chopped
1 zucchini, chopped
½ cup chopped chives or
    scallions
4 cups chicken stock

1 tablespoon chopped lovage
1 teaspoon chopped thyme
1 cup yogurt
1 cup cream
Salt and pepper to taste
Zucchini slivers

Combine potatoes, zucchini, chives, and stock in soup kettle. Bring to a boil, reduce heat, and simmer, partially covered, 15 minutes or until vegetables are tender. Remove from heat, add lovage and thyme, and let sit 5 minutes. Press through food mill. Cool and chill. Stir in yogurt and cream and season with salt and pepper. Garnish with matchstick-size slivers of raw zucchini. *Serves 6-8.*

Fish and Seafood Soups

COLD FISH SOUP

Serve with a well-chilled dry white wine for a delightful summertime lunch.

2 carrots, peeled
1 parsnip, peeled
2 onions, peeled
2 pounds cod or other firm-fleshed white fish, cut into pieces
2 cucumbers, peeled and chopped

1 tablespoon chopped chives
1 tablespoon chopped parsley
1 tablespoon chopped dill
3 tablespoons lemon juice
Salt and pepper to taste
Dill
Lemon slices

Coarsely grate carrots, parsnip, and onions. Combine with cold water to cover in soup kettle and simmer 10 minutes. Add fish, cover, and simmer 20 minutes longer. Remove kettle from heat and cool. Remove fish, discard skin and bones, and cut meat into small pieces. Return fish to kettle. Add cucumbers, chives, parsley, dill, and lemon juice. Season with salt and pepper. Chill thoroughly. Garnish with additional fresh dill and a slice of lemon.   *Serves 4-6.*

COLD LOBSTER SOUP

Also tastes great made with crab meat.

2 tablespoons butter
1 sweet onion, peeled and grated
1 clove garlic, minced
2 carrots, peeled and grated
2 tablespoons chopped parsley
1 teaspoon Dijon mustard

3 cups fish stock
½ pound cooked lobster meat, shredded
1 cup sour cream
Milk
Salt and pepper to taste
Sweet red pepper slivers

Melt butter in skillet and sauté onion, garlic, carrots, and parsley until soft. Cool. Stir mustard into fish stock in large bowl. Add lobster and sautéed vegetables. Puree in blender, several cups at a time. Return to bowl and add sour cream. Stir until blended. Thin with milk to desired consistency. Season with salt and pepper. Garnish with matchstick-size slivers of sweet red pepper.   *Serves 4-6.*

V.
Chowders

Vegetable Chowders

BEAN CHOWDER

Taste and texture will depend on the kind of beans used.

1 cup dry white beans
2 tablespoons chopped celery
   leaves
1 onion, peeled and chopped
¼ pound salt pork or 3 slices
   bacon, diced

2 potatoes, peeled and diced
1 quart milk
Salt and pepper to taste
Chopped parsley

Soak beans overnight in cold water to cover. (Drain or not, as you prefer.) Add cold water to cover, celery leaves, and onion, bring to a boil, reduce heat, and simmer, uncovered, until beans are tender — 30 minutes to 1 hour, depending on the variety. As beans cook, fry salt pork in small skillet until crisp. When beans are done, add salt pork and potatoes. Simmer, partially covered, 15 minutes or until potatoes are tender, adding water if necessary. Stir in milk, season with salt and pepper, and heat thoroughly. Garnish with chopped parsley. *Serves 4.*

LIMA BEAN CHOWDER

Even diehard lima bean haters may succumb to this chowder.

¼ pound salt pork
1 onion, peeled and chopped
4 cups chicken stock
3 potatoes, peeled and
   chopped
1½ cups sliced mushrooms

2 cups fresh lima beans
2 cloves garlic, minced
2 teaspoons chopped parsley
2 cups cream
1 to 2 tablespoons butter
Salt and pepper to taste

Fry salt pork in soup kettle until crisp. Remove with slotted spoon and set aside. Sauté onion in fat until tender. Add stock, potatoes, mushrooms, beans, garlic, and parsley. Simmer, partially covered, 30 minutes. Add cream and butter and heat thoroughly. Season with salt and pepper. Garnish with reserved salt pork. *Serves 6-8.*

CORN CHOWDER I

In summer, use leftover corn-on-the-cob; in winter, frozen, canned, or cream-style corn.

¼ pound salt pork or 3 slices
   bacon, diced
2 onions, peeled and chopped
4 cups chicken stock or water
4 potatoes, peeled and diced

3 cups corn
1 cup cream or milk (omit if
   cream-style corn is used)
Salt and pepper to taste

Fry salt pork in soup kettle until crisp. Remove with slotted spoon and set aside. Sauté onions in fat until golden. Pour in stock. Add potatoes and corn and simmer, partially covered, 15 to 20 minutes or until potatoes are tender. Add cream, season with salt and pepper, and heat; do not boil. Garnish with reserved salt pork.

Serves 4.

CORN CHOWDER II

This version omits salt pork and uses a touch of thyme.

4 cups chicken stock
4 cups water
4 potatoes, peeled and cubed
1 sprig thyme
1 teaspoon celery seed
2 tablespoons butter

1 onion, peeled and chopped
2 cups cream
3 cups cooked corn, canned or
   fresh
Salt and pepper to taste

Combine chicken stock and water in soup kettle. Add potatoes, thyme, and celery seed; bring to a boil, reduce heat, cover, and cook 15 minutes or until potatoes are tender. As potatoes cook, melt butter in skillet. Sauté onion until transparent. When potatoes are done, add onion to stock along with cream and corn. Season with salt and pepper. Heat but do not boil.

Serves 6-8.

CORN CHOWDER III

Carrots and pimiento add pizzazz.

2 large carrots, peeled and grated
1 cup chicken stock
1 quart milk
2 cups (16-ounce can) cream-style corn, or 1½ cups fresh corn and ½ cup heavy cream

3 canned pimientos, finely chopped
2 tablespoons butter
2 tablespoons minced onion
2 tablespoons flour
Salt and pepper to taste

Combine carrots and stock in large saucepan and simmer, uncovered, 5 minutes. Add 3 cups milk, corn, and pimientos and heat. Melt butter in soup kettle. Sauté onion until tender. Sprinkle with flour and slowly add remaining 1 cup milk, stirring with whisk until mixture is smooth. Cook over low heat until thickened. Gradually add carrots and corn mixture, stir, season with salt and pepper, and heat thoroughly. Do not boil.   *Serves 6-8.*

PARSNIP CHOWDER

Parsnips, a mainstay of old-time New England cooking, make a tasty chowder. Serve with corn bread and a green salad.

3 strips bacon, diced
1 onion, peeled and chopped
¼ cup chopped parsley
6 parsnips, peeled and chopped
1 to 2 potatoes, peeled and chopped

2 cups boiling water
3 cups milk
1 cup cream
2 tablespoons butter
2 tablespoons flour
Salt and pepper to taste

Fry bacon in soup kettle until crisp. Remove with slotted spoon and set aside. Sauté onion and parsley in fat until tender. Add parsnips and potatoes, pour in boiling water, and simmer, partially covered, 15 to 20 minutes, or until vegetables are tender. Remove from heat and add milk and cream. Melt butter in saucepan over low heat. Add flour and blend with whisk. Add ½ cup soup liquid and blend until mixture is smooth. Heat soup and slowly stir butter-and-flour mixture back into kettle. Add reserved bacon and increase heat almost to boiling. Season with salt and pepper.   *Serves 6-8.*

POTATO CHOWDER I

Nineteenth-century cookbooks include numerous recipes for potato chowder, undoubtedly developed as an economical yet nutritious meal.

¼ pound salt pork or 3 slices
   bacon, diced
3 onions, peeled and chopped
2 carrots, peeled and chopped

6 potatoes, peeled and cubed
2 quarts chicken stock
Salt and pepper to taste
Chopped parsley

Fry salt pork in soup kettle until crisp. Remove with slotted spoon and set aside. Sauté onions in fat until tender. Add carrots, potatoes, and stock. Simmer, partially covered, 20 minutes or until vegetables are tender. Season with salt and pepper. Garnish with chopped parsley and reserved salt pork. *Serves 6-8.*

POTATO CHOWDER II

Chives or dill perks up this chowder.

¼ pound salt pork, diced
1 onion, peeled and chopped
2 to 3 potatoes, peeled and
   chopped
1 cup corn
1 quart scalded milk

1 tablespoon chopped chives
   or dill
Salt and pepper to taste
3 tablespoons butter
6 soda crackers

Fry salt pork in soup kettle until crisp. Remove with slotted spoon and set aside. Sauté onion in fat but do not brown. In separate pan parboil potatoes 5 minutes in water to cover. Add potatoes to onion, along with 2 cups potato cooking liquid. Cook 15 minutes or until potatoes are tender. Add corn, milk, and chives or dill. Season with salt and pepper and add butter. Place crackers in soup bowls, pour soup over them, and sprinkle with reserved salt pork. *Serves 6.*

TOMATO CHOWDER

Serve in cups as a first course, or in large bowls along with bread as a complete meal.

¼ cup salt pork, diced
1 onion, peeled and sliced
1 potato, peeled and sliced
2 cups water
1 to 1½ cups canned tomatoes,
   chopped
1 teaspoon sugar

Salt and pepper to taste
2 cups cooked corn, canned or
   fresh
2 cups milk
2 tablespoons flour
2 teaspoons cold water

Fry salt pork in soup kettle until crisp. Add onion and sauté until tender. Add potato and water, bring to boil, reduce heat, and cook 15 minutes or until potato is tender. Meanwhile, in separate saucepan combine tomatoes and sugar. Season with salt and pepper and heat just to a boil. When potato is tender add corn and milk to soup. Combine flour and water to form a smooth paste and stir into soup. Add heated tomatoes. Heat thoroughly, but do not boil.

Serves 6.

TOMATO-CORN CHOWDER

Don't be surprised by the delicate pink color of this chowder.

1 quart milk	2 cups cooked corn, canned or
1 cup tomato puree	fresh
2 leaves basil	Salt and pepper to taste
2 stalks celery, chopped	
2 potatoes, peeled and	
chopped	

Combine milk, tomato puree, basil, and celery in soup kettle. Simmer, uncovered, 10 minutes. Do not boil. Remove from heat and strain. Return liquid to kettle; discard solids. Cook potatoes in separate saucepan in boiling water 15 minutes or until tender. Drain. Add potatoes and corn to liquid in kettle, season with salt and pepper, and heat. Do not boil.

Serves 4.

VEGETABLE CHOWDER

Turnips, squash, and other vegetables can also be used in this meatless chowder.

2 onions, peeled	Boiling water
2 carrots, peeled	2 tablespoons butter
2 parsnips, peeled	2 tablespoons flour
4 potatoes, peeled	1 quart milk
8 fresh tomatoes, peeled,	1 cup cream
seeded, and chopped	Salt and pepper to taste

Grate or chop onions, carrots, parsnips, and potatoes. Place in soup kettle along with tomatoes; add boiling water to cover, and simmer, partially covered, 20 minutes or until tender. Melt butter in separate saucepan. Add flour and blend with whisk. Slowly add milk and cream. Stir until smooth. Add milk mixture to kettle and stir until blended. Season with salt and pepper.

Serves 4.

Fish and Seafood Chowders

CLAM CHOWDER I

There are almost as many ways to make clam chowder as there are cooks in New England. Here's one that insists on salt pork for "true" flavor.

¼ pound salt pork, diced
3 onions, peeled and chopped
1½ quarts clam stock and 2
    cups water, or 2 cups
    bottled clam juice and 1½
    quarts water
6 potatoes, peeled and cubed

1 teaspoon chopped thyme
1 teaspoon chopped basil
2 cups cream
2 cups shucked clams,
    coarsely chopped
Salt and pepper to taste

Fry salt pork in soup kettle until crisp. Remove with slotted spoon and set aside. Sauté onions in fat until tender. Add stock, water, potatoes, and herbs. Simmer, partially covered, 15 minutes or until potatoes are just tender. Add cream, clams, and reserved salt pork. Heat slowly. Do not boil.   *Serves 6-8.*

For Mussel Chowder: Substitute mussels for clams and proceed as directed above.

CLAM CHOWDER II

Vermouth and bacon make a distinctive difference.

24 clams
2 cups dry vermouth
2 cups water
3 slices bacon, chopped
1 onion, peeled and chopped

2 potatoes, peeled and
    chopped
2 cups cream
Salt and pepper to taste

Scrub clams and place in soup kettle with vermouth and water. Cover and simmer until shells open. Remove clams with slotted spoon. Strain liquid through double thickness of cheesecloth and set aside. Chop clams and set aside. Clean kettle and fry bacon in it until crisp. Remove with slotted spoon and set aside. Sauté onion in fat until golden. Add reserved stock and potatoes. Simmer, covered, 10 minutes. Add clams and simmer until heated through. Stir in cream and reserved bacon. Season with salt and pepper. Heat and serve.

Serves 4-6.

CLAM CHOWDER III

For a thicker broth, substitute a cup of heavy cream for a cup of the milk.

4 slices bacon	½ teaspoon chopped thyme
1 onion, peeled and chopped	1 cup clam stock
2 stalks celery, chopped	3 tablespoons flour
2 potatoes, peeled and chopped	3 cups milk
	1 cup minced clams

Fry bacon in soup kettle until crisp. Remove with slotted spoon and set aside. Sauté onion and celery in fat. Add potatoes, thyme, and clam stock. Simmer, partially covered, 15 minutes or until potatoes are barely tender. Blend flour and milk and pour into kettle. Stir until blended. Add clams and heat thoroughly. Do not boil. Garnish with reserved bacon, crumbled.

Serves 4-6.

CLAM AND CABBAGE CHOWDER

Be careful never to let the broth boil after adding clams to any chowder.

4 tablespoons butter	1 cup shucked clams
1 head cabbage, cored and cut into 1-inch cubes	5 cups milk
1 cup clam stock (or ½ cup bottled clam juice and ½ cup water)	Salt and pepper to taste

Melt butter in soup kettle and sauté cabbage, stirring gently, over low heat until wilted. Add stock, bring to a boil, reduce heat and simmer 25 minutes, partially covered. (Add additional stock or water if necessary.) Add clams and milk to kettle, stir, season with salt and pepper, and heat thoroughly.

Serves 6-8.

CLAM AND CORN CHOWDER

Two New England favorites in one.

¼ pound salt pork, diced
2 onions, peeled and chopped
2 stalks celery, chopped
2 potatoes, peeled and
    chopped
1 cup clam stock

1 cup cooked corn, canned or
    fresh
2 cups milk
1 cup cream
2 cups minced clams
Salt and pepper to taste

Fry salt pork in soup kettle until crisp. Remove with slotted spoon and set aside. Sauté onions and celery in fat until tender. Add potatoes and stock and simmer, covered, 15 minutes. Add corn, milk, and cream. Simmer, uncovered, 10 minutes. Do not boil. Add clams and heat through. Season with salt and pepper. If desired, garnish with reserved salt pork.   *Serves 4.*

MANHATTAN CLAM CHOWDER

Many New England cooks believe this soup should never darken their dining room doors.

¼ pound salt pork, diced
3 onions, peeled and sliced
2 cups potatoes, peeled and
    chopped
2 cups stewed tomatoes
1 sweet red pepper, cored and
    chopped

2 sprigs thyme
4 cups clam juice or water
1 cup shucked clams
Salt and pepper to taste

Fry salt pork in soup kettle until crisp. Remove with slotted spoon and set aside. Sauté onions in fat until tender. Add potatoes, tomatoes, red pepper, thyme, and clam juice. Bring mixture to a boil, reduce heat, and simmer, partially covered, 20 minutes. Add clams and cook 5 minutes longer. Season with salt and pepper. Garnish with reserved salt pork.   *Serves 4-6.*

FISH CHOWDER

Make with any firm-fleshed white fish, fresh or frozen.

4 pounds white fish, boned
   and cut into chunks
½ cup cider
2 sprigs thyme
Salt and pepper to taste
1 to 2 onions, peeled and
   chopped

1 stalk celery, chopped
1 carrot, peeled and chopped
1 tablespoon chopped green
   or sweet red pepper
1 tablespoon butter
1 cup cream
Chopped parsley

Marinate 2 pounds fish in cider for 1 hour. Combine remaining fish
with cold water to cover, thyme, and salt and pepper in soup kettle.
Simmer, partially covered, 30 minutes. Strain liquid into second
kettle. Discard fish. Add vegetables and cook 10 minutes or until
tender. Meanwhile, drain cider from fish. Melt butter in frying pan
and cook fish over low heat until just tender. Remove broth and
vegetables from heat, gently stir in fish. Heat cream in separate pan
and add to chowder. Garnish with chopped parsley. *Serves 4.*

FISH BALL CHOWDER

*There are many ways to make fish balls, which should be the consistency of
uncooked meat loaf before they are added to the hot liquid.*

1 pound white fish, cleaned
   and skinned
4 cups cold water
1 carrot, peeled and sliced
2 stalks celery, sliced
1 bay leaf
1 sprig parsley
1 cup stale bread crumbs

1 egg, beaten
1 tablespoon butter
2 tablespoons minced onion
4 potatoes, peeled and
   chopped
1 cup cream
Salt and pepper to taste

In soup kettle combine fish, water, carrot, celery, bay leaf, and
parsley. Simmer, partially covered, 15 minutes. Strain. Remove fish
and chop or shred into small bits, discarding any bones. Discard
vegetables. In bowl combine fish with bread crumbs, egg, butter, and
onion. Add a bit of milk if mixture seems dry. Using your hands,
shape into 1-inch balls. Add fish balls and potatoes to kettle with
strained broth. Simmer, partially covered, 15 minutes or until
potatoes are tender. Add cream and season with salt and pepper.
Heat slowly. Do not boil. *Serves 6-8.*

REAL ISLAND FISH CHOWDER

A meal in itself, this chowder should be made a day in advance of serving.

2 cups cold water
2 pounds white fish, fresh or
   frozen
4 onions, peeled and sliced
4 potatoes, peeled and sliced

1 quart milk
1 cup cream
4 tablespoons butter
Salt and pepper to taste

The day before you serve this chowder, bring water to boil in a soup kettle. Add fish and simmer, covered, 10 minutes or until tender. Remove fish, flake into small pieces, and discard skin and bones. Add onions to cooking liquid and simmer, uncovered, 5 minutes. Add potatoes and simmer, uncovered, 10 minutes. Return fish to kettle. Add milk, cream, butter, and salt and pepper. Heat soup slowly for 20 minutes before serving. Stir gently. Serve in large bowls with crackers. *Serves 6-8.*

HADDOCK CHOWDER

You can use any other firm, white fish in this chowder, but haddock has a unique taste.

1½ quarts fish stock
1 onion, peeled and chopped
2 carrots, peeled and chopped
2 to 3 potatoes, peeled and
   chopped
2 tablespoons chopped
   parsley

1 tablespoon chopped basil
1 cup tomato juice or V-8 juice
2 pounds haddock, skinned,
   boned, and cut into 2-inch
   pieces
Salt and pepper to taste

Combine stock, onion, carrots, potatoes, parsley, and basil in soup kettle. Bring to a boil, reduce heat, and simmer, partially covered, 10 minutes. Add tomato or V-8 juice. Bring mixture to a boil again, add haddock, reduce heat, and simmer, partially covered, 10 minutes, or until fish is tender. Season with salt and pepper. *Serves 6.*

SALMON CHOWDER

Use canned salmon, drained and boned, if fresh is not available.

3 strips bacon, diced
1 onion, peeled and chopped
2 carrots, peeled and chopped
1 stalk celery, chopped
3 cups fish stock

1 potato, peeled and chopped
1 pound salmon
1 cup cream
Salt and pepper to taste

Fry bacon in soup kettle until crisp. Remove with slotted spoon and set aside. Sauté onion, carrots, and celery in fat until tender. Add stock and potato, cover, and simmer 10 minutes. Add salmon and simmer 10 minutes longer. Add cream, stir, season with salt and pepper, and heat thoroughly. Garnish with reserved bacon. *Serves 4.*

SCALLOP CHOWDER

Use whole bay scallops, or quartered sea scallops.

2 potatoes, peeled and
  chopped
4 tablespoons butter
2 onions, peeled and chopped
2 cups milk
1½ cups cream

1 pound scallops, fresh, or
  frozen and thawed
Salt and pepper to taste
Chives
Bacon

Steam or boil potatoes until tender. As potatoes cook, melt 2 tablespoons butter in soup kettle and sauté onions until tender. Add milk and cream and simmer gently 15 minutes. Melt remaining 2 tablespoons butter in skillet. Over high heat sauté scallops 3 minutes, turning frequently. Add scallops and potatoes to kettle. Season with salt and pepper. Garnish with fresh chives and crumbled fried bacon. *Serves 4-6.*

Other Chowders

BEEFSTEAK CHOWDER

An unusual recipe from Martha's Vineyard.

¼ pound salt pork, diced
1½ pounds top or bottom
  round steak, cut into 1-inch
  pieces
Flour for dredging

5 cups beef stock
5 potatoes, peeled and
  chopped
1 cup milk
Salt and pepper to taste

Fry salt pork in soup kettle until crisp. Remove with slotted spoon and set aside. Dredge steak in flour and brown slowly in fat in kettle. Add stock, cover, and simmer 1½ hours. Add potatoes, cover, and simmer 20 minutes longer or until tender. Add milk, stir and heat thoroughly, but do not boil. Season with salt and pepper. If desired, garnish with reserved salt pork. (Tastes even better reheated the second day.) *Serves 6-8.*

MARTHA'S VINEYARD CHICKEN CHOWDER

South islanders thicken their chowder slightly, others do not. This version produces a thin broth. For a thicker chowder, mash some of the potatoes and stir into the soup as it heats for the last time.

6-pound fowl
3 quarts cold water
¼ pound salt pork, diced
2 onions, peeled and chopped
8 to 9 potatoes, peeled and
  chopped

2 cups scalded milk or cream
2 tablespoons butter
Salt to taste

The day before you serve this chowder, clean fowl and cut into pieces. Place in soup kettle, cover with cold water, and heat slowly to a boil. Reduce heat and simmer, covered, 3 hours. Remove chicken and cool. Pull meat from bones, discard skin and bones, chop meat, and refrigerate. Cool and chill stock, skim fat off top, and refrigerate.

The following day return stock and chicken to kettle and simmer 10 minutes, partially covered. Fry salt pork in skillet until crisp. Remove with slotted spoon and set aside. Sauté onions in fat until tender. Add onions and salt pork to kettle, along with potatoes, and simmer, partially covered, 15 minutes or until potatoes are tender. Stir in milk and butter and heat. Season with salt.   *Serves 10-12.*

TURKEY CHOWDER

Follow any outdoor winter activities with steaming bowls of this rich, chunky chowder.

2 quarts turkey stock
2 potatoes, peeled and
  chopped
2 carrots, peeled and chopped
1 onion, peeled and chopped
2 stalks celery, chopped

1 tablespoon chopped parsley
1 cup milk
1 cup cream
1 cup diced, cooked turkey
  meat
Salt and pepper to taste

Combine stock, potatoes, carrots, onion, celery, and parsley in soup kettle. Simmer, partially covered, 15 minutes or until vegetables are tender. Add milk, cream, and turkey. Season with salt and pepper. Heat thoroughly.   *Serves 6-8.*

EGG CHOWDER

The appearance of the eggs is important. For bright yellows, place eggs into cold water immediately after boiling and peel them when they are cool.

¼ pound salt pork, diced
5 potatoes, peeled and
  chopped
3 cups water

2 cups cream
2 tablespoons butter
5 to 6 hard-boiled eggs, sliced
1 tablespoon dill or parsley

Sauté salt pork in soup kettle until crisp. Do not remove. Add potatoes and water and simmer, covered, 15 minutes or until potatoes are tender. Heat cream in separate pan and add to kettle along with butter and eggs. Sprinkle in dill or parsley and heat gently.   *Serves 4-6.*

CHEESE CHOWDER

Just the thing on a frosty fall evening, followed by hot apple pie.

4 potatoes, peeled and
  chopped
5 carrots, peeled and chopped
1 onion, peeled and chopped
2 cups chicken stock
4 tablespoons butter

3 tablespoons flour
2 cups milk
2 cups grated sharp cheddar
  cheese
Salt and pepper to taste
Chopped parsley

Combine potatoes, carrots, onion, and stock in soup kettle and simmer, partially covered, 15 minutes. As vegetables cook, melt butter in saucepan. Add flour and stir until blended. Slowly add milk, stirring with a whisk, until mixture is smooth. Stir in cheese and cook over low heat until melted. Season with salt and pepper. Slowly add cheese mixture to vegetables and stock, stirring over low heat until blended. Garnish with chopped parsley.   *Serves 4-6.*

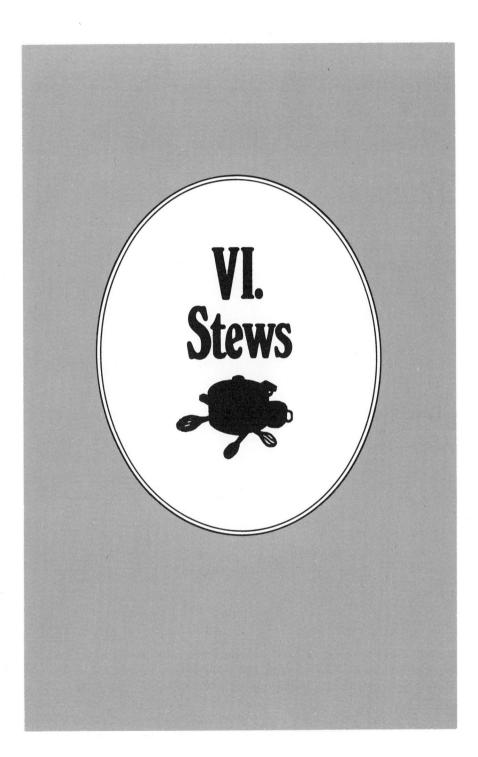

VI.
Stews

Meat Stews

BEEF AND BEAN STEW

Try snap beans, peas, and other vegetables in this stew. By adding them at the end you can preserve their flavors, as well as their textures and colors.

¼ pound salt pork, diced
4 onions, peeled and chopped
2 cloves garlic, minced
2 pounds stew beef, cubed
1 can (28 ounces) tomatoes and juice

2 cups beef stock
2 cups fresh green beans, cut into 1-inch pieces
½ cup boiling water
Salt and pepper to taste

Preheat oven to 325°. Fry salt pork in oven-proof casserole until crisp. Remove with slotted spoon. Sauté onions and garlic in fat. Add beef and stir over low heat until all sides are brown. Add tomatoes and stock. Cover and bake 2½ hours. When meat is tender, simmer beans, uncovered, in boiling water 5 minutes. Drain, add to stew, and stir. Season with salt and pepper.   *Serves 4.*

BEEF AND EGGPLANT STEW

Zucchini can take the place of eggplant in this dish.

4 tablespoons oil
2 pounds stew beef, cubed
4 onions, peeled and chopped
2 cloves garlic, minced
6 ripe tomatoes, peeled and chopped
½ cup dry white wine

4 cups chicken stock
2 sprigs parsley
3 eggplants, peeled and chopped
2 sweet red peppers, cored and chopped
Salt and pepper to taste

Heat oil in Dutch oven and brown beef over low heat, turning so all sides are done. Add onions and garlic and cook 5 minutes. Add tomatoes, wine, stock, and parsley. Cover and simmer 1 hour. Add eggplants and simmer 1 hour longer. Add peppers and simmer 20 minutes or until beef is tender. Season with salt and pepper. *Serves 6.*

BEEF AND MUSHROOM STEW

Green olives provide extra color for this fragrant dish.

2½ pounds beef chuck, cubed
2 cloves garlic, minced
2 carrots, peeled and sliced
1 onion, sliced
1 bay leaf
2 sprigs thyme
2 sprigs rosemary

2 cups dry red wine
½ pound salt pork, diced
3 tablespoons flour
2 tablespoons butter
½ pound mushrooms, sliced
¼ cup sliced green olives
Salt and pepper to taste

Combine beef, garlic, carrots, onion, bay leaf, thyme, rosemary, and wine in large bowl. Cover and marinate overnight in refrigerator. Stir once or twice. Fry salt pork in oven-proof casserole until crisp. Remove with slotted spoon and set aside. Preheat oven to 350°. Strain meat and vegetables, reserving marinade. Cook meat and vegetables in salt pork fat 10 minutes, stirring until meat is browned on all sides. Sprinkle with flour, stir to coat evenly, and add marinade. Continue stirring until mixture is smooth. If necessary, add water or water and wine until meat is covered with liquid. Bake, covered, 1 hour. Remove meat from sauce; strain out and discard vegetables. Return meat and sauce to casserole. Melt butter in small frying pan and sauté mushrooms 2 minutes. Add mushrooms to meat and sauce and bake, covered, 30 minutes. Add olives, stir, and cook 5 minutes. Season with salt and pepper. If desired, garnish stew with reserved salt pork. *Serves 4-6.*

CHILI

Although this stew did not originate in New England, it has earned a place in almost every Northern home.

1 tablespoon oil
1 onion, peeled and chopped
1 clove garlic, minced
2 stalks celery, chopped
1 pound ground beef
2 cups (16-ounce can) stewed
 tomatoes or peeled fresh
 tomatoes, with juice

1 cup (8-ounce can) tomato
 sauce
2 cups (15-ounce can) cooked
 kidney beans
Salt and pepper to taste

Heat oil in Dutch oven. Sauté onion, garlic, and celery until soft. Add beef and brown. Drain off excess fat. Add tomatoes and tomato sauce, cover, and simmer 30 minutes. Add beans and simmer until heated. Season with salt and pepper. Serve with crackers or bread, or on top of baked potatoes. *Serves 4.*

HOT CHILI

Here's one of the spicier versions of this stew. Omit hot pepper and cumin for a milder dish.

3 tablespoons oil
2 pounds rump roast, diced
2 yellow onions, peeled and
  chopped
1 hot pepper, cored and
  chopped

1 clove garlic, minced
1 cup tomato sauce
1 tablespoon ground cumin
2 tablespoons chili powder
1 teaspoon sage
Salt and pepper to taste

Heat oil in Dutch oven and brown meat evenly on all sides. Remove meat and set aside. Sauté onions, hot pepper, and garlic until tender. Return meat to pot, add tomato sauce and cold water to cover. Simmer, covered, 2 hours. Add remaining ingredients, cover, and simmer 1 hour longer. Season with salt and pepper.   *Serves 4-6.*

JOE BOOKER STEW

Top this basic beef stew with dumplings and have on a cold winter night.

½ pound salt pork, diced
3 onions, peeled and sliced
1½ pounds lean stew beef,
  cubed
Flour for dredging
3 cups beef stock
3 sprigs parsley

1 bay leaf
2 sprigs summer savory
1 sprig thyme
2 to 3 potatoes, peeled and
  sliced
4 carrots, peeled and sliced
Salt and pepper to taste

Fry salt pork in heavy skillet until crisp. Remove with slotted spoon and set aside. Sauté onions in fat until tender and remove to Dutch oven. Dredge beef in flour and brown in hot fat, turning to cook all sides. Place in Dutch oven with onions and beef stock. Tie herbs in cheesecloth bag and add to pot. Heat to a boil, reduce heat, cover, and cook 1 hour. Add potatoes and carrots and cook 20 minutes longer or until vegetables are tender. Remove herbs. Season with salt and pepper. If desired, place dumplings on stew.   *Serves 4-6.*

POT-AU-FEU

Make a day ahead, or start it on the morning of the day you plan to serve it, to allow plenty of time for chilling.

3 pounds beef brisket	¼ cup chopped parsley
2 marrow bones	1 sprig thyme
3 quarts cold water	1 bay leaf
2 onions, peeled and chopped	8 whole baby carrots
2 leeks, thinly sliced	8 new potatoes
4 carrots, peeled and sliced	Salt and pepper to taste

Trim as much fat as possible from brisket. Combine meat with bones and water in Dutch oven. Heat until gently simmering. Add onions, leeks, carrots, parsley, thyme, and bay leaf. Cover and simmer 2 hours. Discard vegetables. Remove meat and cut into serving pieces. Discard bones. Pour stock into large bowl, cool to room temperature, refrigerate, return meat and stock to Dutch oven and reheat. As stock is heating, steam or boil carrots and potatoes in separate pans until tender. Add to stew. Season with salt and pepper. *Serves 6-8.*

PIONEER BEEF STEW

Complete the meal with mashed potatoes and biscuits.

½ cup dry lima beans	½ cup beef stock
½ cup flour	1 can (14½ ounces) tomatoes,
1 teaspoon salt	chopped and undrained
½ teaspoon pepper	1 teaspoon salt
1½ pounds stew beef, cubed	1 bay leaf
2 tablespoons oil	1 onion, peeled and chopped
1 onion, peeled and chopped	4 carrots, peeled and sliced
1 green pepper, cored and	3 stalks celery, sliced
chopped	Parsley

Soak beans overnight in water to cover. Drain. Combine flour, salt, and pepper and dredge beef in mixture. Heat oil in Dutch oven and brown beef over low heat on all sides. Add onion, green pepper, stock, tomatoes, salt, and bay leaf. Cover and simmer 1 hour. Add soaked, drained beans, additional onion, carrots, and celery. Cover and simmer 30 minutes longer. Remove bay leaf and garnish with parsley. *Serves 4.*

PEPPERPOT

Although sold today in many supermarkets, tripe isn't universally popular. If you're not interested in trying it, substitute a pound of stew beef and brown in oil before combining with vegetables.

1 pound fresh tripe
1 pound veal knuckle
3 quarts cold water
8 whole cloves
12 peppercorns
6 sprigs parsley
2 sprigs marjoram
3 leaves basil
2 sprigs thyme

2 green peppers, cored and chopped
3 onions, peeled and chopped
2 beets, peeled and chopped
2 parsnips, peeled and chopped
4 tablespoons butter
½ cup uncooked rice
Salt and pepper to taste

Wash tripe and cut into cubes. Place in Dutch oven with knuckle and add water. Bring to a boil and boil 15 minutes. Reduce heat, skim, cover, and simmer 1½ hours. Tie cloves, peppercorns, and herbs in cheesecloth, add to pot, cover again, and cook 1 hour more. Remove cheesecloth and discard. Sauté vegetables in butter for 5 minutes. Add to Dutch oven along with rice, cover, and simmer 30 minutes. Remove knuckle. Cool, skim, and reheat. Season with salt and pepper. *Serves 6-8.*

VEAL STEW

Serve this aromatic stew with garlic bread and a cucumber salad.

1 teaspoon oil
1 pound veal stew meat, cubed
1 onion, peeled and chopped
1 clove garlic, minced
½ cup dry white wine
2 tablespoons tomato paste
1 tablespoon lemon juice
3 cups chicken stock
1 teaspoon oregano

½ teaspoon rosemary
2 potatoes, peeled and quartered
8 small white onions, peeled
4 carrots, peeled and sliced
2 stalks celery, sliced
1 teaspoon chopped parsley
Salt and pepper to taste

Heat oil in Dutch oven and brown veal evenly on all sides. Add onion and garlic. Cook 5 minutes. Add wine, tomato paste, lemon juice, stock, oregano, and rosemary and stir until smooth. Cover and simmer 35 minutes. Add remaining ingredients and simmer, covered, 20 minutes or until vegetables are tender. Season with salt and pepper. *Serves 6.*

VEAL AND CAULIFLOWER STEW

Beef can be substituted for veal in this easy-to-make stew.

2 tablespoons butter
3 onions, peeled and chopped
1 pound veal stew meat, cubed
Flour for dredging
4 cups veal or beef stock
6 peppercorns

1 bay leaf
½ head cauliflower, cut into
   small pieces
3 tablespoons chopped chives
Salt and pepper to taste
¼ cup sherry (optional)

Melt butter in Dutch oven and sauté onions until tender. Remove onions and set aside. Dredge veal in flour and brown evenly on all sides in remaining butter. Return onions to Dutch oven, add stock, peppercorns, and bay leaf. Cover and simmer 30 minutes. Add cauliflower and chives, cover, and simmer 15 minutes or until veal and cauliflower are tender. Season with salt and pepper. Add sherry if desired and stir until blended. Serve in soup bowls.   *Serves 4.*

VEAL AND LEEK STEW

Like many other stews, this seems to taste better when reheated the day after it is made.

4 pounds veal stew meat,
   cubed
Flour for dredging
4 tablespoons butter
4 leeks, whites and ⅓ green
   parts, sliced
1 onion, peeled and sliced
4 stalks celery and leaves,
   sliced

2 green peppers, cored and
   sliced
4 carrots, peeled and sliced
3½ cups beef stock
½ cup dry white wine
2 egg yolks
Salt and pepper to taste

Preheat oven to 350°. Dredge veal in flour. Melt butter in oven-proof casserole and sauté veal, leeks, and onion over low heat until brown. Add celery, green peppers, carrots, stock, and wine; cover and bake 45 minutes or until veal is tender. Spoon out ½ cup stew liquid and cool slightly. Add to egg yolks, blend with whisk, and pour mixture back into stew. Season with salt and pepper. Reheat but do not boil.
                                                        Serves 4-6.

IRISH LAMB STEW

Mint jelly and hot biscuits are a must with this traditional New England dish.

3-pound lamb shoulder
4 cups cold water
2 onions, peeled and sliced
2 stalks celery, chopped
Flour for dredging
2 tablespoons butter
1 cup beef stock
2 sprigs parsley

1 bay leaf
3 to 4 onions, sliced
1 to 2 potatoes, peeled and chopped
4 carrots, peeled and cut into 1-inch pieces
Salt and pepper to taste

Trim meat from bones, cube, and set aside. Combine bones, water, onions, and celery in Dutch oven. Simmer, partially covered, 30 minutes. Strain and reserve liquid. Discard bones and vegetables. Cool and skim fat from top of liquid. Dredge meat in flour. Melt butter in frying pan and brown meat on all sides. Place in Dutch oven, add stock, reserved liquid, parsley, and bay leaf. Simmer gently, partially covered, 1 hour. Remove bay leaf and parsley. Add additional onions, potatoes, and carrots and cook, partially covered, 30 minutes longer. Season with salt and pepper.   *Serves 6-8.*

SPRING LAMB STEW

Make when new potatoes, baby carrots, and tiny tender peas are available.

4 tablespoons butter
3 pounds boned lamb shoulder, cut into 1-inch cubes
2 tablespoons flour
1 clove garlic, minced
1 sprig rosemary
1 bay leaf
3 sprigs parsley

½ cup dry white wine
3 cups beef stock
12 small, whole new potatoes, unpeeled
12 baby carrots, peeled
12 small, whole white onions
1 cup fresh peas
½ cup boiling water
Salt and pepper to taste

Preheat oven to 325°. Melt butter in skillet and brown lamb over low heat. Place browned meat in oven-proof casserole. Over low heat sprinkle flour over lamb and stir gently until blended. Add garlic, rosemary, bay leaf, and parsley. Pour in wine and stock, stirring to form a smooth sauce. Cover casserole and simmer in oven 1 hour. Add potatoes, carrots, and onions to stew (make sure there is ample liquid; add more stock if necessary to cover vegetables) and cook 30 minutes longer. As vegetables cook, place peas in small saucepan, add boiling water and simmer, covered, 5 minutes. (Don't cook the peas any longer or they will lose their lovely color.) Drain, add to stew, season with salt and pepper, and serve.   *Serves 4-6.*

GOULASH

There is no single way to make this meat stew, which usually includes veal or pork (beef will also work), and cream to thicken and enrich the gravy. Try homemade spaetzle to give the meal a special touch, or use packaged egg noodles if time is short.

3 tablespoons butter
4 yellow onions, peeled and
   sliced
2 cloves garlic, minced
2 pounds boned pork, cubed
1 tablespoon paprika
   (Hungarian if available)

3 cups veal or chicken stock
2 teaspoons caraway seed
4 green or sweet red peppers,
   cored and sliced
1 cup sour cream or yogurt
Salt and pepper to taste

Preheat oven to 350°. Heat butter in oven-proof casserole and sauté onions and garlic until tender. Do not brown. Add pork and brown slowly, stirring so all sides are evenly done. Sprinkle with paprika and stir until blended. Add stock and caraway seed and stir until smooth. Cover and bake 30 minutes. Add peppers and bake, covered, 15 to 20 minutes longer, or until pork is tender. Remove from oven. Stir in sour cream or yogurt, and season with salt and pepper. Serve with spaetzle or noodles.   *Serves 6.*

PORK STEW I

Serve this colorful stew with garlic bread or baking powder biscuits and a grapefruit/avocado salad.

1 tablespoon butter
2 pounds boneless pork shoulder, cubed
1 tablespoon flour
1½ cups beef stock
4 carrots, peeled and cut into 1-inch lengths
2 onions, peeled and sliced

5 ripe tomatoes, peeled and chopped, or canned (10 ounces), chopped
1 teaspoon salt
½ teaspoon caraway seed
1 head cabbage, coarsely shredded
Chopped parsley

Melt butter in Dutch oven. Brown pork and stir until blended. Sprinkle with flour and stir to coat evenly. Add stock and stir until blended. Add carrots, onions, tomatoes, salt, and caraway seed. Bring to a boil, reduce heat, and simmer, covered, 30 minutes. Add cabbage. Simmer, covered, 30 minutes longer, or until pork and vegetables are tender. Garnish with chopped parsley.   *Serves 4-6.*

PORK STEW II

Fix anytime, for any occasion.

2 tablespoons oil
2 pounds pork, cubed
4 onions, peeled and chopped
1 clove garlic, crushed
2 cups chicken stock

2 carrots, peeled and chopped
1 green pepper, cored and chopped
1 teaspoon chopped marjoram
Salt and pepper to taste

Heat oil in Dutch oven and brown pork on all sides. Mix in onions and garlic and cook 5 minutes over low heat. Add stock, bring to a boil, reduce heat, cover, and simmer 1 hour. Add carrots, green pepper, and marjoram and simmer, partially covered, 15 minutes longer. Season with salt and pepper.   *Serves 4-6.*

PORK AND VEGETABLE STEW

Also try fresh zucchini, summer squash, or carrots.

2 tablespoons oil
1 onion, peeled and chopped
1 green pepper, cored and
  chopped
2 pounds boneless pork,
  cubed
1 tablespoon chopped
  rosemary

5 ripe tomatoes, peeled and
  chopped
½ cup chicken stock
1 eggplant, peeled and cubed
Salt and pepper to taste
Chopped parsley

Heat oil in Dutch oven and sauté onion and pepper until tender.
Add pork and cook over medium heat, turning so all sides are
brown. Add remaining ingredients except parsley, reduce heat,
cover, and simmer 1 hour. (If stew becomes too watery after first
half hour of cooking, simmer remaining half hour uncovered.) Garnish with chopped parsley.   *Serves 4-6.*

SAUSAGE STEW

Use hot sausage for a spicier dish.

2 tablespoons butter
2 pounds sweet Italian
  sausage, sliced
2 tablespoons flour
4 cups beef stock
1 large can (28 ounces) peeled
  plum tomatoes, with juice

1 teaspoon chopped basil
1 teaspoon oregano
3 small zucchini, thinly sliced
½ cup small pasta, uncooked
Salt and pepper to taste

Melt butter in Dutch oven and brown sausage over low heat. Drain
off fat. Sprinkle with flour and stir until blended. Add stock,
tomatoes, basil, and oregano. Bring to a boil, reduce heat, and
simmer 30 minutes, partially covered. Add zucchini and pasta and
simmer 10 minutes longer or until tender. Season with salt and
pepper. (If preferred, cook pasta in separate saucepan, add to stew,
and stir.)   *Serves 4-6.*

Poultry, Fish, and Seafood Stews

CHICKEN MULLIGATAWNY

One theory claims this recipe made its way into New England via the sea captains who discovered it in their travels to India.

1 pound chicken parts
1 onion, peeled and sliced
4 cups cold water
3 tablespoons butter
3 tomatoes, peeled and
   chopped
1 carrot, peeled and sliced
1 stalk celery, sliced
1 green or sweet red pepper,
   cored and sliced

2 tart apples, cored and sliced
2 tablespoons flour
1 teaspoon dry mustard
2 sprigs parsley
2 teaspoons curry powder
Cooked rice
Salt and pepper to taste

Combine chicken, onion, and water in Dutch oven. Cover and simmer 30 minutes. Remove chicken, discard skin and bones, chop meat, and set aside. Cool stock, chill, and skim fat from top. Reheat stock in Dutch oven with chicken. Melt butter in heavy skillet. Sauté tomatoes, carrot, celery, pepper, and apples until soft. Sprinkle with flour, stir until blended. Pour 1 cup hot stock into vegetables, stir until smooth, and add vegetables to Dutch oven. Simmer, partially covered, 10 minutes. Add mustard, parsley, and curry powder, stir until blended, and simmer, partially covered, 15 minutes longer. Season with salt and pepper. Serve with rice. *Serves 6.*

BRUNSWICK STEW

This stew used to be made with squirrel meat.

5 tablespoons butter
3 onions, peeled and sliced
¼ cup flour
2 teaspoons rosemary
1 teaspoon salt
1½ pounds chicken pieces
   (thighs, legs, wings)

2 cups chicken stock
2 tomatoes, peeled, seeded,
   and chopped
1 cup cooked corn, canned or
   fresh

Heat 2 tablespoons butter in Dutch oven. Sauté onions until tender. Remove with slotted spoon. Combine flour, rosemary, and salt in bowl or plastic bag. Coat chicken with flour mixture. Melt remaining 3 tablespoons butter in Dutch oven. Brown chicken over moderate heat. Add stock, bring to a boil, reduce heat, cover, and simmer 30 minutes. Add sautéed onions, tomatoes, and corn. Cover and simmer 10 to 15 minutes longer. *Serves 4.*

CHICKEN STEW

Serve topped with dumplings.

4-pound stewing chicken, cut
   into pieces
2 onions, peeled and sliced
1 stalk celery, sliced
1 bay leaf
6 peppercorns
Cold water

3 tablespoons butter
2 tablespoons flour
3 potatoes, peeled and diced
2 carrots, peeled and diced
2 cups fresh green beans, cut
   into 1-inch pieces
Salt and pepper to taste

Combine chicken, onions, celery, bay leaf, and peppercorns in Dutch oven. Add cold water to cover. Simmer, covered, 2 hours. Remove chicken and cool. Pull meat from bones and chop. Discard skin and bones. Cool broth, chill, and skim. Return to Dutch oven with chopped chicken. Heat to simmer. Melt butter in small skillet, add flour, and stir to form smooth paste. Slowly add to pot and stir until well blended. Add potatoes, carrots, and beans. Simmer, partially covered, 15 minutes or until vegetables are tender. Season with salt and pepper. *Serves 6.*

GIBLET STEW

Serve with a fruit salad.

2 pounds chicken giblets
(hearts, gizzards, livers)
and necks, skinned
2 quarts chicken stock
2 stalks celery, chopped
2 onions, peeled and chopped

2 tablespoons chopped
parsley
½ cup uncooked rice
Salt and pepper to taste
Chopped parsley

Combine gizzards, hearts, necks, and stock in Dutch oven and simmer, covered, 30 minutes. Add livers and cook 15 minutes longer. Drain. Cool stock, chill, and skim fat from top. Trim gristle from gizzards and chop with hearts and livers. Pick meat from necks. Return stock and meat to pot. Bring to a boil, add celery, onions, and parsley, and simmer, partially covered, 10 minutes. Add rice, reduce heat, cover, and simmer 20 minutes longer, or until rice is cooked. Season with salt and pepper. Garnish with chopped parsley. *Serves 6-8.*

BOUILLABAISSE

There are many ways to make this patriarch of fish stews. Serve all ingredients in large bowls or pass the fish around on a platter. Scallops and lobster can also be included.

¼ cup olive oil
2 onions, peeled and chopped
1 clove garlic, minced
1 bay leaf
6 tomatoes, peeled and
chopped
1 cup fish stock
1 cup dry white wine
Pinch saffron
3 tablespoons chopped
parsley

1 pound white fish, cleaned,
skinned, and cut into
serving pieces
24 raw, shucked clams or
mussels
24 small or 12 large raw
shrimp, cleaned
Salt and pepper to taste

Combine oil, onions, garlic, and bay leaf in Dutch oven. Cover and simmer 10 minutes. Add tomatoes, stock, wine, saffron, and parsley, cover, and simmer 20 minutes longer. Add fish, clams or mussels, and shrimp, cover, and cook 15 minutes. Season with salt and pepper. *Serves 4-6.*

CLAM STEW

Try this or your own favorite recipe for oyster stew, but substitute clams for the oysters. The taste is great, the cost reasonable.

2 tablespoons butter
2 stalks celery, chopped
2 cups milk
2 cups cream
1 quart steamed clams,
    cleaned

Salt and pepper to taste
Butter
Dash of paprika

Melt butter in saucepan. Sauté celery until tender. Do not brown. Add milk, cream, and clams. Heat slowly until clams are heated through. Do not boil. Season with salt and pepper. Top each serving with a bit of butter, sprinkle with paprika, and serve immediately.

Serves 4.

CLAM AND TOMATO STEW

Mussels, lobster meat, or white fish can also be added to this fragrant stew.

¼ cup olive oil
4 to 6 cloves garlic, minced
6 tomatoes, peeled and
    chopped
2½ cups tomato juice
3 cups dry white wine
4 cups fish stock

4 dozen small whole raw
    shrimp, cleaned
¼ cup chopped parsley
2 cups small whole steamed
    and shucked clams
Salt and pepper to taste

Heat oil in Dutch oven. Sauté garlic until tender. Add tomatoes, tomato juice, wine, and stock. Bring to a boil. Add shrimp and parsley and simmer, partially covered, until shrimp turns pink. Add clams and heat thoroughly. Season with salt and pepper.   *Serves 6-8.*

PORTUGUESE FISH STEW

There are many versions of this dish, which, here, is built in layers.

2 cloves garlic, minced
4 tablespoons oil
2 cups dry white wine
¼ teaspoon pepper
1 tablespoon cumin powder
6 onions, peeled and sliced
3 pounds firm white fish,
    cleaned and cut into pieces
¼ pound squid, chopped
    (optional)

½ cup chopped parsley
5 potatoes, peeled and sliced
6 ripe tomatoes, peeled and
    sliced
4 sweet red or green peppers,
    cored and sliced into 2-inch
    strips
Salt to taste
Fresh chopped parsley

In small mixing bowl beat together garlic, oil, wine, pepper, and cumin. Line a large, oven-proof casserole with a layer of onions. Add a layer of fish, a layer of squid, sprinkle with some parsley, add a layer of potatoes, a layer of tomatoes, and a layer of peppers. Sprinkle with half the garlic and oil mixture. Repeat layers, ending with onions. Sprinkle with remaining garlic and oil. Cover and simmer 30 minutes. Season with salt. Garnish with chopped parsley.

Serves 6-8.

HALIBUT STEW

For a complete meal, serve with warm bread or rolls and sliced tomatoes.

4 tablespoons butter
¼ cup chopped shallots
2 cups chicken stock
½ cup dry white wine
¼ cup Madeira

2 tablespoons tomato paste
2 pounds halibut, cut into
    serving pieces
Salt and pepper to taste
Chopped parsley or dill

Melt butter in Dutch oven. Sauté shallots until soft. Add stock, wine, Madeira, and tomato paste. Stir until smooth. Add fish. Season with salt and pepper. Bring just to a boil, reduce heat, and simmer, partially covered, 20 minutes. Garnish with chopped parsley or dill.

Serves 4-6.

LOBSTER STEW I

As many New Englanders will tell you, the simpler a lobster stew is, the better it tastes.

3 tablespoons butter
1 onion, peeled and chopped
2 cups milk
2 cups cream
1 cup cooked lobster meat
    chunks

2 tablespoons sherry, or more
    to taste
Salt and pepper to taste
Paprika

Melt butter in saucepan. Sauté onion until tender. Slowly add milk, cream, and lobster meat. Heat but do not boil. Add sherry, season with salt and pepper, and garnish with paprika.   *Serves 4.*

LOBSTER STEW II

Cook slowly in a heavy saucepan or double boiler.

5 tablespoons butter
½ cup sherry
1 cup cooked chopped lobster
    meat
½ cup sliced mushrooms
1 small onion, peeled and
    minced

½ green pepper, cored and
    chopped
1 tablespoon flour
2 egg yolks
2 cups cream
Salt and pepper to taste

Melt 2 tablespoons butter in saucepan. Add sherry and bring to a boil. Add lobster and remove from heat. In separate saucepan melt remaining 3 tablespoons butter. Sauté mushrooms, onion, and green pepper until soft. Sprinkle with flour and stir until blended. Drain sherry from lobster and add to sautéed vegetables. Heat to simmer. Beat egg yolks and cream, add ¼ cup of hot sherry, blend with whisk, and return mixture to saucepan. Stir mixture slowly over low heat. Add lobster and heat. Season with salt and pepper.   *Serves 4.*

OYSTER STEW

A good oyster stew is little more than oysters warmed in cream, milk, or a combination of the two. The secret is to heat the liquid slowly; if it boils, oysters toughen.

24 fresh oysters, with their liquor
2 tablespoons butter
2 cups milk
2 cups cream
Dash of Tabasco
Salt and pepper to taste

Combine oysters and their liquor in top of double boiler. Cook over boiling water until edges of oysters begin to curl. Add butter and stir gently until melted. In separate pan heat milk and cream. Add to oysters along with Tabasco. Season with salt and pepper. Stir slowly until heated through. Serve immediately, with oyster crackers.

Serves 4.

SQUID STEW

Serve with hot pickles and steamed rice.

3 tablespoons butter
3 tablespoons oil
2 to 3 onions, peeled and chopped
3 pounds cleaned squid, fresh or frozen, sliced
1½ quarts cold water
1 can (6 ounces) tomato paste
¼ cup chopped parsley
2 tablespoons vinegar
1 teaspoon salt
¼ teaspoon pepper
3 to 4 potatoes, peeled and cubed

Melt butter in Dutch oven and add oil. Sauté onions until tender. Add squid and sauté 5 minutes. Add water, tomato paste, parsley, vinegar, salt, and pepper. Simmer, uncovered, 10 minutes. Add potatoes, cover, and simmer 20 minutes or until tender. Stir occasionally to prevent sticking.

Serves 4-6.

Other Stews

POTATO STEW I

Serve this tasty alternative to mashed or baked potatoes with meat loaf or roast chicken.

3 strips bacon, diced
2 onions, peeled and chopped
3 potatoes, peeled and
  chopped
1 parsnip or turnip, peeled
  and chopped
1 cup chicken stock
1 tablespoon butter
1 tablespoon flour
½ cup milk
1 cup cream
Salt and pepper to taste

Fry bacon in Dutch oven until crisp. Remove with slotted spoon and set aside. Sauté onions in fat until tender. Add other vegetables, cover with stock, and simmer, partially covered, 20 minutes or until tender. As vegetables cook, in separate saucepan melt butter over low heat. Add flour, blend with whisk, and gradually add milk, stirring constantly to form a smooth sauce. Add to stew when vegetables are tender. Stir until smooth, add cream, and heat. Season with salt and pepper. Garnish with reserved bacon.   *Serves 4.*

POTATO STEW II

Fresh herbs make a big difference in this stew. Chives or dill may be substituted for lovage.

2-inch cube salt pork, diced
1 onion, peeled and chopped
1 clove garlic, minced
3 cups chicken stock

2 tablespoons tomato paste
1 tablespoon chopped lovage
4 potatoes, peeled and cubed
Salt and pepper to taste

Fry salt pork in Dutch oven until crisp. Remove with slotted spoon and set aside. Sauté onion and garlic in fat until tender. Add stock, tomato paste, and lovage. Stir until smooth. Add potatoes, cover, and simmer 15 minutes or until potatoes are tender. Season with salt and pepper. If desired, garnish with reserved salt pork.   *Serves 4.*

RATATOUILLE

This popular combination of fresh summer or fall vegetables can be served as a stew. With less liquid it becomes a side dish to a main meal.

4 tablespoons oil
3 onions, peeled and chopped
2 green or sweet red peppers,
   cored and chopped
1 clove garlic, minced
1 eggplant, peeled and
   chopped
4 small zucchini, sliced
6 ripe tomatoes, peeled and
   chopped, or 2 cups canned
   plum tomatoes, chopped,
   with juice

¼ cup chopped parsley
3 basil leaves, chopped
Salt and pepper to taste
1 cup canned chick-peas,
   drained
Mozzarella cheese

Heat oil in oven-proof casserole. Sauté onions, peppers, and garlic over low heat until soft. Do not brown. Add eggplant, zucchini, tomatoes, parsley, and basil. Turn heat down very low, cover, and cook 30 minutes. Stir several times. Season with salt and pepper. Add chick-peas and simmer, covered, 10 minutes longer. (Check amount of liquid. If stew is swimming, spoon off excess, leaving ample broth.) Cover top with slices of mozzarella. Place under broiler until cheese is bubbly and brown.   *Serves 6-8.*

VII.
Croutons,
Dumplings,
Noodles, and
Baked Goods

CROUTONS

Experiment with this and the following two recipes to discover which you prefer with your favorite soups, chowders, and stews.

Cut crusts from slices of stale bread. Spread slices with softened butter. Cut into cubes, place on baking sheet, and toast in 250° oven. Turn and brown slowly on all sides. Or, fry unbuttered bread cubes in hot fat, drain, and sprinkle with salt.

GARLIC CROUTONS

Remove crusts from several slices of stale bread and cut into cubes. Melt 2 tablespoons butter in small skillet and sauté 1 crushed clove garlic 5 minutes. Discard garlic. Sauté bread cubes on all sides until brown. Drain and sprinkle with salt.

HERB CROUTONS

Chop equal amounts of fresh chervil, parsley, and chives. Mix with several tablespoons softened butter, spread on slices of bread, and cube. Bake in 250° oven until lightly toasted. Turn so all sides are brown.

DUMPLINGS

This recipe makes enough to serve with 2 quarts soup or stew.

2 cups flour	2 tablespoons shortening or
1 tablespoon baking powder	lard
½ teaspoon salt	¾ cup milk

Sift dry ingredients and work in shortening. Add milk to make soft dough. Drop dough by spoonfuls onto top of hot soup or stew. Cook, uncovered, 10 to 12 minutes. Cover and cook 10 minutes longer. *Makes approximately 12.*

CORNMEAL DUMPLINGS

Try these as an alternative to corn bread.

1½ cups white cornmeal	1 teaspoon salt
½ cup flour	1 egg, beaten
1 tablespoon baking powder	½ to ¾ cup milk

Sift together dry ingredients. Add egg, then gradually pour in enough milk to make a soft dough. Drop dough by spoonfuls onto hot soup or stew. Cook 10 minutes, uncovered. Cover and cook 10 minutes longer. *Serves 6.*

NOODLES FOR SOUP

Homemade noodles are heavier than those you buy at the store, and taste best if they are sliced very thin.

Beat 1 egg until light yellow. Add a pinch of salt and enough flour to form a stiff dough. Roll out until very thin and dredge with flour to keep from sticking. Roll up tightly, jelly-roll fashion, and beginning at one end, shave down as if you are cutting cabbage for cole slaw. Or, pinch off small bits of dough with your thumb and forefinger. Add to soup and simmer 10 minutes. *Makes 1 cup.*

SPAETZLE

These thick noodles are not difficult to make, but you may need help with a step: one person to hold the colander while the other presses the dough through the holes.

2 cups flour	½ to ¾ cup milk
3 eggs, beaten	Salt and pepper to taste

Place flour in mixing bowl. Add eggs and mix until blended. Slowly add milk, mixing constantly, to form a stiff dough. Sprinkle with salt and pepper. Fill a soup kettle ⅔ full of water and bring to a boil. Hold colander over kettle (wear heavy, long mitts to avoid burns from steam), pour spaetzle dough into colander, and press through the holes with a rubber spatula, forcing spaetzle into boiling water. When noodles rise to the surface, they are done. Drain, spoon into a bowl, top with butter, and serve with stew or goulash. *Serves 6.*

CHEESE CRACKERS

Serve with any soup.

Lightly butter saltines, soda crackers, or sea biscuits and spread on baking sheet. Sprinkle with grated cheddar cheese. Broil several minutes or until cheese is melted.

CHEESE STICKS

Try these instead of the usual crackers with chowders or soups.

1 cup grated cheddar cheese	1 teaspoon salt
1 cup flour	1 egg, beaten
1 teaspoon baking powder	2 tablespoons milk, or more

Preheat oven to 450°. Combine cheese, flour, baking powder, and salt. Add egg and milk to make a stiff dough. Roll out ¼ inch thick on floured board. Cut into thin strips 4 to 5 inches long. Place on greased baking sheet and bake 10 minutes. *Makes 2-3 dozen.*

BAKING POWDER BISCUITS

Hot from the oven, these will complement any soup or stew.

2 cups flour	4 tablespoons lard or
3 teaspoons baking powder	shortening
1 teaspoon salt	½ to ¾ cup milk

Preheat oven to 450°. Sift together flour, baking powder, and salt. Cut in lard. Add milk, stirring slowly to make a soft dough. Turn mixture out onto floured surface, knead lightly several times, and shape into a ball. Roll out to ¼- to ½-inch thickness. Cut with round or heart-shaped cookie cutters or the rim of a juice glass. Bake 10 to 15 minutes on ungreased baking sheet. *Makes 12 biscuits.*

CHEESE BISCUITS

Simple to make, and especially good with vegetable soups.

2 cups flour
2 teaspoons baking powder
1 teaspoon salt
1 cup grated cheddar cheese

4 tablespoons lard or
   shortening
¾ cup milk

Preheat oven to 450°. Sift together flour, baking powder, and salt. Blend in cheese and lard. Add milk, stirring slowly to make a soft dough. Drop by spoonfuls onto greased baking sheet. Bake 10 to 15 minutes.   *Makes 15-20.*

CHEESE ROLLS

Serve with vegetable soups or stews.

2 cups flour
2 teaspoons baking powder
1 teaspoon salt
4 tablespoons lard or
   shortening

1 cup milk
3 tablespoons melted butter
1 to 1½ cups grated cheddar or
   Swiss cheese
Salt and pepper to taste

Preheat oven to 425°. Sift together flour, baking powder, and salt. Blend in lard. Slowly add milk and stir to make a soft dough. Turn onto floured board and knead lightly, several times. Roll out into thin rectangle. Brush dough with melted butter, sprinkle cheese over dough, and season with salt and pepper. Starting at one long side, roll dough up, jelly-roll fashion. With a sharp knife cut into 1-inch slices. Place slices on greased baking sheet and bake 15 minutes or until light brown.   *Makes 2 dozen.*

POPOVERS

These make any soup, chowder, or stew extra special.

1 cup flour
½ teaspoon salt
2 eggs, beaten

1 tablespoon melted butter
1 cup milk

Preheat oven to 350°. Sift together flour and salt. Add eggs, butter, and milk and stir until smooth. Pour into greased muffin pans or custard cups and bake 20 minutes. Increase heat to 450° and bake 10 minutes longer. Turn heat off and let popovers sit 10 minutes in oven.   *Makes 10-12.*

CORN GEMS

Serve with clam chowder.

2 cups fresh uncooked corn,
   cut from cobs
¼ cup milk
2 eggs

2 cups flour
2 teaspoons baking powder
1 teaspoon salt

Preheat oven to 400°. Press raw corn through food mill. Add milk and eggs and beat until well blended. Sift together flour, baking powder, and salt and add to wet ingredients. Mix well. Grease muffin pans and heat in oven. Drop batter into hot pans, filling ⅔ full, and bake 25 minutes. *Makes 12-18.*

CARAWAY MUFFINS

A tasty accompaniment for most soups, chowders, or stews.

2 cups flour
3 teaspoons baking powder
1 tablespoon sugar
1 teaspoon salt

2 eggs
1 cup milk
4 tablespoons melted butter
1 tablespoon caraway seed

Preheat oven to 400°. Sift together flour, baking powder, sugar, and salt. In separate bowl beat together eggs, milk, butter, and caraway seed. Add wet ingredients to dry and mix well. Fill greased muffin pans half full of batter. Bake 15 to 20 minutes. *Makes 12-14.*

CORN BREAD

Superb with chili, Portuguese stews, or chowders.

1 cup cornmeal
1 cup flour
3 teaspoons baking powder
1 tablespoon sugar

1 teaspoon salt
1 egg, beaten
1½ cups milk
4 tablespoons melted butter

Preheat oven to 425°. Sift together cornmeal, flour, baking powder, sugar, and salt. Add egg, milk, and butter and beat until well mixed. Pour into greased 8-inch skillet or 8-inch-square pan. Bake 25 minutes. Cool and cut into squares. *Makes approximately 12 pieces.*

CORNMEAL MUFFINS

A nice change from corn bread; the batter can also be baked in corn stick pans.

1½ cups flour
2 teaspoons baking powder
1 teaspoon salt
1 cup cornmeal

2 eggs, beaten
1 cup milk
3 tablespoons melted butter

Preheat oven to 425°. Sift together flour, baking powder, and salt. Add cornmeal. In separate bowl combine eggs, milk, and butter. Slowly add wet ingredients to dry, stirring until blended. Spoon mixture into greased muffin pans and bake 25 to 30 minutes.

Makes 12.

Index